KITCHENS AND BATHROOMS

TIME
LIFE
BOOKS

This volume is part of a series offering home
owners detailed instructions on repairs,
construction and improvements which they can
undertake themselves.

HOME REPAIR
AND IMPROVEMENT

KITCHENS AND
BATHROOMS

BY THE EDITORS OF
TIME-LIFE BOOKS

TIME-LIFE BOOKS
AMSTERDAM

TIME-LIFE BOOKS

EUROPEAN EDITOR: Kit van Tulleken
Assistant European Editor: Gillian Moore
Design Director: Ed Skyner
Photography Director: Pamela Marke
Chief of Research: Vanessa Kramer
Chief Sub-Editor: Ilse Gray

HOME REPAIR AND IMPROVEMENT

EDITORIAL STAFF FOR KITCHENS AND BATHROOMS
Editor: Philip W. Payne
Designer: Anne Masters
Text Editors: Mark M. Steele (principal), Lee Greene
Writers: Margaret Fogarty, Steven J. Forbis, Stuart
Gannes, Kumait Jawdat, Brian McGinn, Mary Paul,
Lydia Preston, Brooke C. Stoddard
Associate Designer: Abbe Stein
Art Associates: George Bell, Michelle Clay, Kenneth E.
Hancock, Richard Whiting
Editorial Assistant: Eleanor G. Kask

EUROPEAN EDITION
Series Director: Jackie Matthews
Writer/Researcher: Charles Boyle
Designers: Paul Reeves (principal), Debbie Martindale
Sub-Editors: Frances Dixon, Hilary Hockman

EDITORIAL PRODUCTION
Chief: Jane Hawker
Production Assistants: Alan Godwin, Maureen Kelly
Picture Co-ordinator: Peggy Tout
Editorial Department: Theresa John, Debra Lelliott

THE CONSULTANTS: Richard Pilling, the plumbing consultant for the
book, is a lecturer in Plumbing and Mechanical Services at Erith
College of Technology, in Belvedere, Kent. He has also worked as a
heating engineer in industry.

Leslie Stokes was a self-employed carpenter and joiner for seven years,
specializing in purpose-made joinery and internal fittings. Since 1976
he has taught in the building department at the Hammersmith
and West London College.

Robert F. Cox, the general consultant for this book, has owned a kitchen
and bathroom remodelling business and worked in the field as a
contractor for more than 25 years. He is chairman of the national Council
of Certified Kitchen Designers in the United States and has written
several manuals for bathroom and kitchen builders. He lectures widely
at industry gatherings and teaches courses in bathroom contracting
for professional designers.

Contents

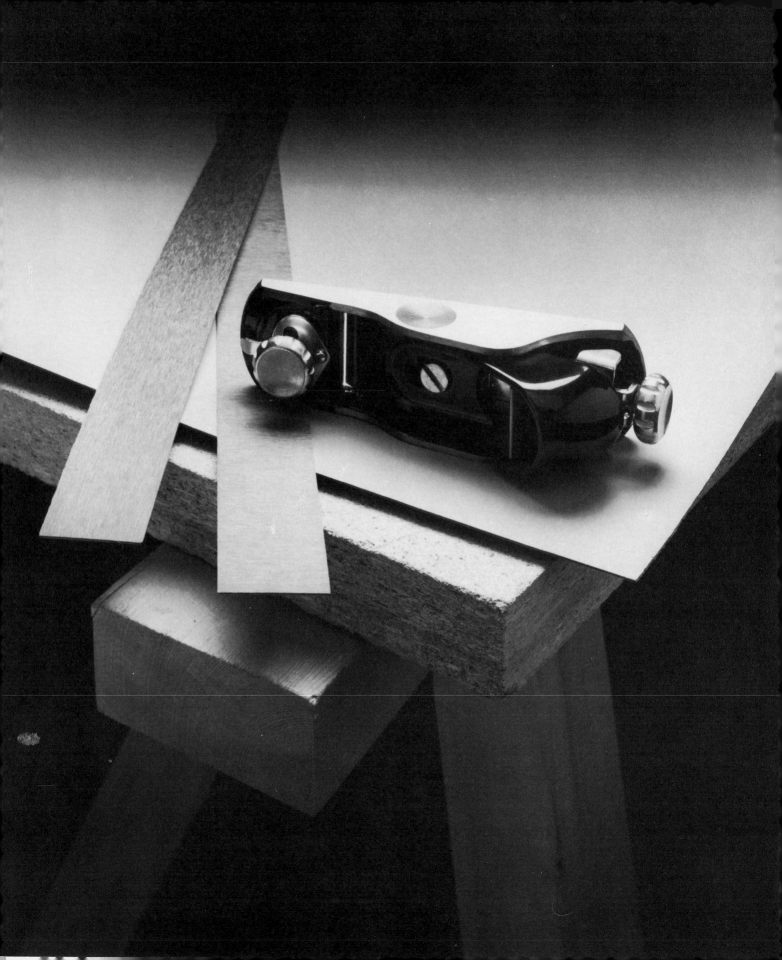

A laminating tool to make neat edges. For neat trimming of plastic laminate on worktops and vanity units, a block plane is the simplest and most convenient tool. The surface sheet is bonded to the chipboard core with contact adhesive and trimmed flush with the sides. The edge strips are applied and then trimmed, and finally the sharp joints between the laminate edges are bevelled with the plane held at a 45-degree angle.

No rooms are more used—and abused—than kitchens and bathrooms. Their floors carry the heaviest traffic; their cabinets are attacked by heat, moisture, acids and alkalis; their walls are splashed by cleaning agents and grease, and drenched by water and steam. These factors must be considered when renovating or building such rooms, for they affect every step of the work from planning to carpentry, plumbing and electrical installations *(Chapters 2, 3 and 4)*. But the major consideration is the surface—floors, walls and worktops. In kitchens and bathrooms their coverings are special. They have to be.

A large selection of materials is now available to protect and beautify the exposed surfaces of these difficult rooms. Improved adhesives enable an amateur to practise the ancient art of tile setting *(pages 22–29)* or the modern one of plastic lamination *(pages 30–35)*. For both kitchens and bathrooms, the most practical and least expensive floor coverings are resilient materials such as rolled sheet vinyl *(pages 14–19)*.

The main surface of a work space offers the widest choice of all. An ideal worktop material would be stainproof, impervious to moisture, scratch resistant, unaffected by heat, slightly resilient, good to look at and reasonably priced. Every popular material combines some, but not all, of these qualities. Ceramic tile is hard, moistureproof and heat resistant—but the crevices between tiles collect dirt and breakages can easily occur on the hard surface. Plastic laminates are resilient, non-porous and resistant to grease and household chemicals—but they are easily damaged by knife scratches or hot pans. Factory-made worktops with finished surfaces are readily available, but mastery of the techniques described in this chapter will enable you to choose and install a surface material—or range of materials—appropriate to your needs.

The choice of materials for walls and floors depends partly on economics and partly on aesthetics, but also on practical considerations of durability, application methods, comfort and safety. In areas where tough, impervious surfaces are not essential, another factor is worth weighing: noise. Ceramic tile, plastic laminate and non-cushioned vinyl bounce sounds to increase the din in rooms that are already very noisy. Wallpaper or paint, while hardly sound absorbent, add less to noise than these materials. On floors, carpeting with a dense pile of nylon fibres designed especially for kitchens and bathrooms creates a feeling of luxury and warm comfort.

The most time-consuming task in laying new coverings is often the preparation of old surfaces *(pages 8–13)*. Walls and floors in good condition may need only to be thoroughly cleaned, but old coverings must usually be stripped off, and repairs—which can range from the patching of damaged areas to the complete replastering of a wall or re-laying of a subfloor—are often necessary. Damp surfaces must be made waterproof and uneven surfaces made level. Careful preparation is always worthwhile, however, because the quality of any wall or floor covering is only as good as the surface on which it is laid.

Preparing for New Walls and Floors

Renovating a kitchen or bathroom wall or floor begins with creating a clean, sound, level subsurface. This usually involves removing or repairing the existing finish—plaster, plasterboard, tile, linoleum or wood—and then applying a new one.

If you are planning substantial alterations to a room, preparing a wall may require building additional framing *(pages 94–97)* or installing special waterproof wallboard round a bath or shower. In most cases, however, you will need only to patch the holes or cracks in your wall, reseat any popped nails, reattach loose plasterboard and perhaps remove wallpaper before applying a new finish.

Cracks, small holes and shallow depressions in plaster-faced brick or masonry walls can be filled with spatchel, an oil-based filler. Deep holes must be patched with undercoat plaster followed by a finishing coat *(opposite page, below)*. Remove any big bulges with hammer and cold chisel—protecting your eyes with goggles—and patch the resulting hole. If plaster has deteriorated badly, strip it all off, then re-plaster, or replace it with plasterboard attached to a framework of battens.

On timber-frame walls, holes in plasterboard can be repaired by attaching scrim cloth to provide a key for finishing plaster *(opposite page, above)*. For larger areas of damage, cut out the affected plasterboard from stud to stud and nail in replacement pieces. On older types of partition wall, in which plaster is laid over a framework of lathes attached to timber studs, carefully cut out any damaged lathes and make good the wall with patches of plasterboard.

Floors take more punishment than walls and often require more extensive preparation. The subfloor over which a finish floor is laid may be either concrete or timber; there may also be an underlayment of plywood, chipboard or hardboard between the subfloor and the finish floor, and all surfaces need to be in good condition before a new finish is laid. (Quarry tiles and, in very old houses, stone flags may sometimes be found beneath a finish floor.)

Concrete subfloors may be either suspended on reinforced beams laid across steel girders or, at ground level, laid direct to earth over a hardcore base. A direct-to-earth concrete subfloor laid without a damp-proof membrane between the con-crete slab and the final screed may well be affected by rising damp. This can usually be cured by treating the floor with a waterproofing epoxy or bitumen compound. Uneven surfaces with irregularities of less than 10 mm should be coated with self-levelling latex cement smoothing compound, which dries in 24 hours and can be applied to any type of subfloor *(page 10)*.

Timber subfloors usually consist of square-edged or tongue and groove boards laid across joists, but in modern houses sheets of chipboard or plywood may be used instead. Loose floorboards must be refixed with cut floor brads, lost-head nails or countersunk 38 mm screws. Damaged boards or sheets must be patched or replaced completely *(pages 10–13)*. Irregularities of less than 3 mm can be sanded down with an electric floor sander, but if the entire surface is worn or uneven, the subfloor should be coated with self-levelling compound or covered with plywood, chipboard or hardwood.

Plywood, chipboard and hardboard for underlayment is available in 2400 by 1200 mm or 1200 by 1200 mm sheets. With joists up to 500 mm apart, use 15.5 mm plywood or 18 mm chipboard; with joists 600 mm apart, use 18 mm plywood or 22 mm chipboard. Hardboard must be at least 3 mm thick. Unless pre-sealed, chipboard should be primed before laying; hardboard, which expands in contact with moisture, must be wetted and left overnight before fixing.

Make sure the existing finish flooring does not conceal decay below. Search for loose or broken tiles, lifting and curling seams, buckling, dampness, odours, discoloration or other signs of moisture under sinks and basins and round baths, dishwashers and W.C.s.

Without adequate ventilation, dampness can cause rot in timber subfloors. Wet rot affects timber only, but dry rot can spread rapidly to brickwork and other structural materials. Anywhere the floor feels soft or yielding, remove a section of finish flooring and probe the area with a bradawl or screwdriver—timber that yields easily is probably affected by rot. Check for blocked air bricks, ruptured damp-proof membranes or other possible contributory factors; under a well-ventilated suspended subfloor, you should be able to feel a cool air flow on your hand. To treat wet or dry rot, seek professional advice.

Removing ceramic tiles. Wear safety goggles when removing ceramic tiles from a wall or a floor. Begin where you can work the edge of a cold chisel under the edge of a tile. To make a start, you may have to smash one tile with a hammer and chisel out the fragments. Then work on the edges of adjoining tiles with gentle taps on the chisel. By working gently you minimize damage to the subsurface and avoid much patching and filling later. Handle broken pieces carefully; they can be razor-sharp.

When repairing a tiled surface before laying a new surface over it, fill the spaces left by broken or missing tiles with spatchel. Reattach loose tiles with adhesive *(page 28)*.

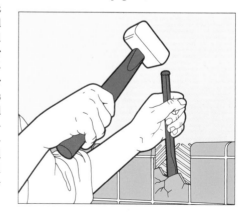

Patching Holes in Plasterboard

1 **Enlarging the hole.** Using a trimming knife, score a line about 13 mm round the outside of the hole. Scrape away the paper covering and a thin layer of plaster inside the scored line to make a recessed area. Cut a piece of scrim cloth to fit into the recessed area—two pieces of cloth will be needed if the diameter of the area is greater than the width of the scrim cloth.

2 **Attaching the scrim cloth.** Using the corner of a plasterer's trowel, fill the recessed area with a thin coat of finishing plaster. Attach the scrim cloth by pressing it into the wet plaster. Leave the plaster to dry for about 10 minutes.

3 **Adding the finishing coat.** Apply a coat of finishing plaster over the scrim cloth. Leave the plaster until it has become pale in colour and almost dry, then smooth down the surface with the plasterer's trowel, using light upward and downward strokes. If the plaster is very stiff, dampen the surface by flicking water on to it with a paintbrush to make it workable.

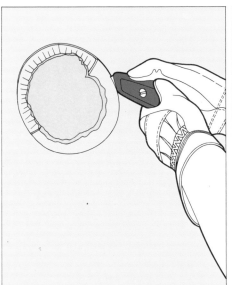
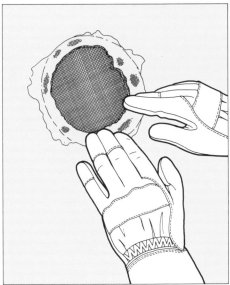
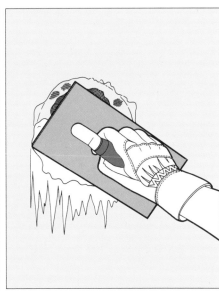

Patching Deep Holes in Plaster

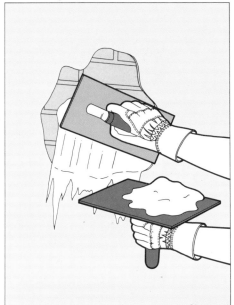
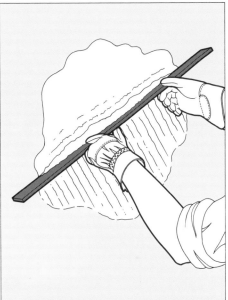
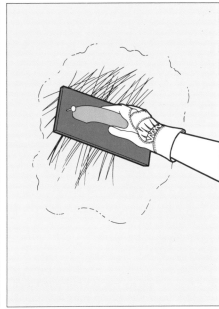

1 **Applying the first coat.** Clean out the hole thoroughly with a stiff brush. Mix a batch of undercoat plaster. Using a plasterer's trowel, apply freshly mixed undercoat plaster to the exposed brickwork with upward, sweeping strokes until the plaster is just proud of the surrounding wall surface.

2 **Striking off.** Leave the plaster for about 10 minutes, until it feels dry to the touch. Use a straight piece of scrap timber to strike off the plaster proud of the wall surface. Work from the bottom of the hole upwards, using a zigzag motion; keep the ends of the piece of scrap timber pressed firmly against the sound surfaces surrounding the hole.

3 **Scratching the undercoat.** Allow the undercoat plaster to dry until pale, then scratch it vigorously to provide a key for the finishing plaster—a suitable tool for this is a wooden float with a nail driven through it *(above)*. Apply a thin coat of finishing plaster. When almost dry, smooth it down with the trowel; dampen the surface if necessary to make it workable.

Levelling and Patching Floors

Removing floor moulding. Before you add or subtract a layer of finish flooring, remove any quadrant moulding attached to the floor along the bottom of the skirting. Beginning near the centre of the wall, prise out the moulding with an old screwdriver far enough to admit the end of a crowbar. Working along the wall in both directions, dislodge the quadrant moulding, dropping in small wood wedges as you go, until the moulding is free. If you wish to replace or reposition the skirting boards, remove them in the same way.

Work carefully with any moulding that you intend to re-use. If the moulding should start to split, drive the nail that is splitting it on through with a nail punch.

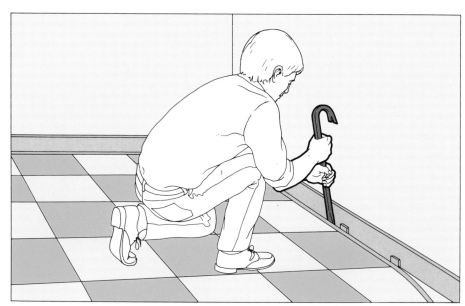

Preparing an old floor surface. Before laying any covering over an existing floor, clean the floor thoroughly. All dirt and wax must be removed; a floor sander will speed the job. Rebond loose vinyl tiles by applying a hot iron, protecting the tile surface with an old towel *(right)*. If heat fails to reactivate the adhesive, lift the tile, scrape up the old adhesive and reset the tile with new adhesive. Fill the spaces left by missing or broken tiles with latex cement smoothing compound.

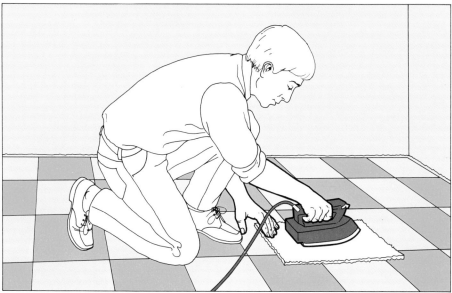

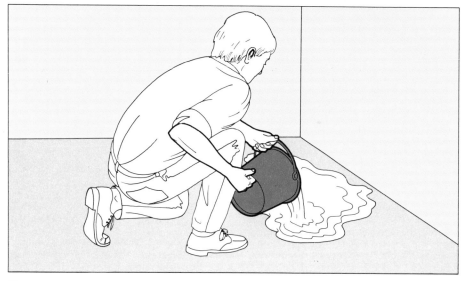

Levelling an uneven subfloor. Clean the subfloor surface thoroughly and check that it is dry. Following the manufacturer's instructions, mix self-levelling compound in a bucket with water to a smooth, creamy consistency. Beginning at the corner of the room farthest from the doorway, pour the compound directly on to the floor. As you work backwards across the floor towards the doorway, spread the compound over the floor surface with a steel float. Leave the compound to set for the time recommended by the manufacturer.

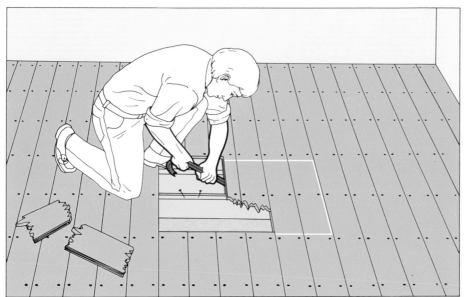

Patching tongue and groove floorboards. Cut each damaged floorboard at the centre of the nearest joist. Saw the tongue off one of the damaged boards and prise the board out with a flooring bolster or, as shown, with a crowbar. Then prise out the remaining damaged boards, leaving a rectangular hole and exposing the tongue edge of a board at one side. Trim off the tongue. Replace the damaged boards with new boards cut to size or with a plywood patch the same thickness as the floorboards.

Floorboards are usually 18 mm thick and can be replaced with 18 mm plywood. In an old house the boards may be of an odd thickness and you may have to shim beneath the plywood patch in order to make it flush.

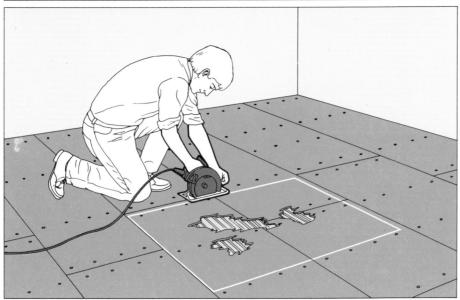

Patching a plywood or chipboard subfloor. Poke a chisel or screwdriver through a soft spot in the damaged area to determine the depth of the subfloor, then set the blade of a circular saw to that depth. Cut out a segment of subfloor, cutting back to the centre of the nearest joist on the sides of the damaged area that run parallel to the joists. Cut out a replacement piece of plywood or chipboard the same thickness as the existing flooring, and nail or screw down this patch on to the exposed joists.

Installing underlayment. Arrange the sheets of underlayment in a staggered pattern of whole sheets and fractions of sheets that avoids the alignment of joints. To allow for expansion, separate the sheets from one another by about 2 mm and leave about 3 mm between the outside edges of the underlayment and the walls. Fasten each sheet with annular ring-shanked nails, lost-head nails or screws; they should be spaced 100 mm apart over the whole surface of the sheet and set 9 mm in from the edges.

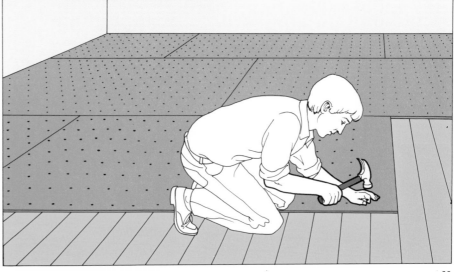

Replacing a Damaged Subfloor

A timber subfloor that is badly worn or extensively damaged must be replaced entirely. In a bathroom, you will probably need to disconnect and remove the bath *(pages 90–91)*, but if the subfloor underneath is in good condition, leave it intact and remove the old flooring round it.

Begin by removing the skirting boards and finish flooring *(page 10)*. Then, starting at one side of the room, remove the old floorboards. When working with tongue and groove, saw off the tongue of the first board, then prise up the boards with a crowbar or bolster *(page 11, top)*. Lay a sheet of plywood or chipboard across the exposed joists as a working platform. When all the boards have been removed, check the joists and underfloor area for decay; if you find any signs of rot, seek professional advice.

When laying new tongue and groove floorboards *(below)*, ensure they are fitted the correct way up; each tongue should be slightly nearer the bottom than the top. Force the boards together tightly to make a draughtproof surface. Cut the boards carefully to length; at end-to-end joints, the end of each board must lie across the centre of a joist, so that there is enough room for both boards to be nailed down.

Flooring-grade chipboard or plywood can also be used to make a smooth, sound subfloor *(opposite)*. Tongue and groove chipboard sheets are available in thicknesses of 18 mm, which is adequate for most rooms, and 22 mm, which should be used if joists are more than 450 mm apart; the most common sheet size in the UK is 2440 by 610 mm. For kitchens and bathrooms, use specially treated, moisture-resistant chipboard.

Once secured, tongue and groove sheets are difficult to lift. Before the sheets are laid, therefore, make access panels over any pipes or cables that may need to be reached. Cut the panels so that two of the sides coincide with joist centres, and install bearers between the joists to support the other two sides. Secure the panels with screws so that they can be easily removed.

Laying New Tongue and Groove Boards

1 **Forcing the boards together.** Butt the tongue of the first board tightly against the wall; make sure that the board is not warped. Using cut floor brads or lost-head nails, nail the board along the wall side only. Lay the next five boards in place, slotting the tongue of each into the groove of the previous board. Place paired wedges cut from scrap wood at intervals of about 1 metre along the side of the last board to be laid, and temporarily nail blocks of wood on to the joists to hold the wedges in place. Using two hammers, knock the wedges against each other to close up all the gaps between the boards *(right)*; alternatively, use a single hammer to strike each wedge in turn. Nail the boards to the joists, using two cut floor brads or lost-head nails in each board; nail the last board along one side only, so that the tongue of the next board can be slotted into the groove. Remove the wedges and holding blocks and continue laying the next five boards. Repeat this process until the joists are covered to within two board-widths of the wall.

2 Fitting the last board. Lay the last full-width board in position, then cut a strip off another board to fill the gap between the full-width board and the wall. Fit the strip into the gap, slotting its tongue into the groove of the full-width board. Using a hammer, drive wooden wedges between the strip and the wall to force the boards tightly together *(right)*, then nail both boards down on the joists. The small gap between the wall and the board will be covered by the skirting board.

Laying Chipboard Sheets

1 Marking the joist lines. Draw marks on the wall above the centre of each joist at both sides of the room. As you lay each chipboard sheet, use a straightedge and pencil to extend the joist lines across the sheet as a nailing guide *(right)*.

Lay the chipboard sheets in a staggered pattern, with the shorter sides of each sheet running parallel to the joists. Joints between adjacent tongue and groove sheets do not have to lie directly over joists.

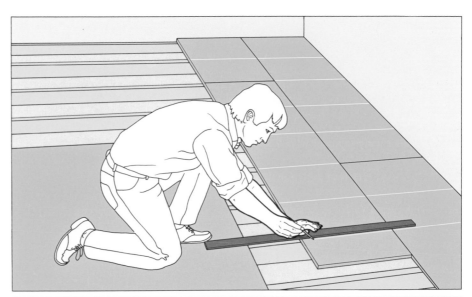

2 Securing the sheets. Using 60 mm lost-head nails or 50 mm No. 8 countersunk screws spaced at intervals of about 200 mm, secure the chipboard to the joists along the pencil lines. Where the ends of two sheets meet at a joist, stagger the nails or screws to prevent the joist splitting.

Rolled Flooring: Seamless and Easy on the Feet

Years ago, rolled sheets of flooring were made of only one material—linoleum. Nowadays, the material is almost certain to be rolled vinyl, which is flexible, hardwearing and easy to maintain and install.

Rolled vinyl flooring is available either in single-layer sheets, usually 2 mm thick, or in sheets with a cushion backing of high-density PVC foam. The latter variety is softer and more sound-absorbent, but may become permanently marked by furniture legs supporting heavy loads or by stiletto heels. Both types of vinyl sheet are available in a wide range of colours and designs, and in widths of 2, 3 and 4 metres; in most household kitchens and bathrooms, the wide widths eliminate the need for seams between adjoining sheets. The design is either printed directly on to the vinyl or pressed through the vinyl to give an embossed surface.

Vinyl can be laid on all types of subfloor except for solid concrete floors without a damp-proof membrane. Before laying, ensure that the floor surface is clean, dry and level *(page 8)*; drive home any protruding nails in timber underlayment with a hammer and nail punch. Remove quadrant moulding round the walls *(page 10)*; for a neat finish, you can also remove skirting boards and replace them with cove moulding after the vinyl is laid *(page 20)*. All movable items such as refrigerators and washing machines should be taken out of the room before the vinyl is laid; when returning these appliances to the finished room, push them back on a piece of old carpeting or on vinyl offcuts to avoid scoring or cutting the newly laid floor.

As the first step in an installation, make a plan of the floor, marking the dimensions. Add 100 mm to each wall to allow for accurate trimming. If sheets need to be joined, note the width of the pattern repeat and add this to your plan. Cut a sheet of vinyl roughly to the dimensions indicated by your plan, then re-roll the sheet with the pattern inwards and the shorter dimension as the width of the roll. To allow the vinyl to adjust to room temperature and to attain maximum flexibility, leave the roll for 24 hours at a temperature of about 18°C. If possible, stand the roll upright: a roll laid on its side may "flatten" while it is resting, causing ripples in the surface of the vinyl when it is laid.

When laying vinyl in a small room that contains obstructions such as a W.C. or a basin pedestal, the best way to ensure an accurate fit is to make a paper template as a guide for cutting vinyl *(below)*. If you need more than one sheet of vinyl to cover a room, or if you have no convenient area in which to lay out the vinyl for transferring a template pattern, follow the procedure described on pages 16–19 for rolling out the vinyl in the room and then trimming. Fixed units set away from a wall require special care *(page 18)*.

Double-sided adhesive tape is usually adequate for sticking down vinyl and allows for easy removal of the vinyl if you wish to replace it later. For permanent fixing, use the adhesive recommended by the vinyl manufacturer *(page 18)*. If there is no threshold in the doorway of the room, the final step in the installation is to fit a metal edging strip, which provides the simplest transition from the new vinyl flooring you have laid to the floor covering in an adjacent room *(page 21)*.

Cutting Vinyl from a Template

1 **Laying out the paper.** Spread out a sheet of stiff paper—such as the felt paper used for carpet underlayment—to cover the entire floor surface; tape several sheets together if necessary. Roughly cut the paper to fit round the walls and any projections such as pipes or a W.C. pedestal, leaving a gap of 12 to 20 mm all round, then secure the paper with drawing pins or small weights.

2 **Making the template.** Use a pair of compasses set at about 37 mm to trace the outline of the walls and any projections on to the paper. Keep the point of the compasses pressed firmly into the junction of the floor with the walls and projections, and hold the pencil at right angles to the object being traced *(right, above)*. Use a ruler and pencil to square off pipes and other small circular projections *(right, below)*: butt the ruler against the pipe on three sides and draw lines along the outer edge of the ruler. Take care not to move the paper on the floor during the tracing.

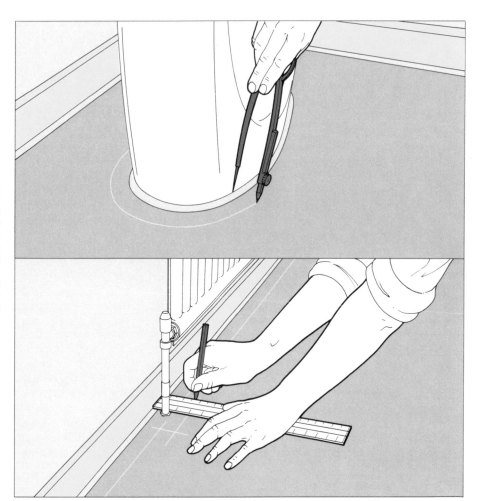

3 **Transferring the outline.** Roll out a sheet of vinyl in a convenient space and lay the paper template on top of it. Move the template until the pattern on the vinyl is square to the doorway. Ensure that both the vinyl and the template are lying absolutely flat, then secure the template to the vinyl with masking tape.

Using the compasses set at the same distance as before, move the point along the template lines to transfer the outline on to the vinyl with the pencil. Keep the compasses at right angles to the lines on the template. Use the ruler to help you trace straight lines *(right)*.

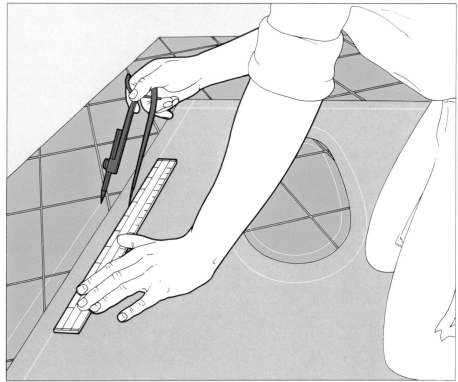

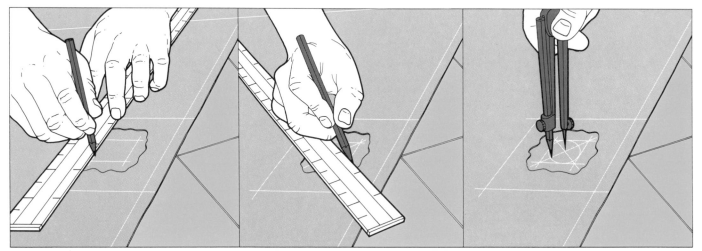

4 **Marking holes for pipes.** Where the template has been squared off around the pipes and any other small circular projections, align one edge of the ruler against each of the lines on the template in turn and trace pencil lines along the ruler's other edge on to the vinyl. Draw a fourth line as necessary to complete the square *(above, left)*. Join the corners of the square with diagonal lines to find the centre *(above, centre)*. Set compasses with the point on the centre and the pencil on one side—a distance equal to the radius of the pipe—and draw a circle on the vinyl *(above, right)*.

5 **Laying the vinyl.** Remove the template from the vinyl sheet. Cut the vinyl along the lines you have traced with a trimming knife; where it is necessary to cut in from the edge of the vinyl for projecting objects, cut along lines in the vinyl pattern if possible so that the cut will not show. Roll up the vinyl with the pattern facing in, then unroll it on the floor to be covered. Smooth the vinyl carefully into corners and round projections, and trim where necessary.

6 **Securing the vinyl with tape.** Cut double-sided adhesive tape to the length of one wall, then fold back about 150 mm of vinyl along the wall. Remove the backing paper from one side of the tape and stick the tape on the floor as close as possible to the wall. Remove the backing paper from the top face of the tape, then press the vinyl firmly into place with a roller or block of wood. Secure the edges of vinyl round the remaining walls and around projections in the same way; where you have cut in from the walls for projecting objects, centre the tape beneath the seam.

Laying Vinyl in a Large Room

1 **Unrolling the sheet.** Unroll the vinyl sheet parallel to the longest unobstructed wall. Manoeuvre the sheet to leave a trimming allowance of 100 mm running up each wall, and check that the pattern is square to the doorway. Sweep the vinyl with a soft broom, applying firm pressure to ensure that the vinyl is lying absolutely flat.

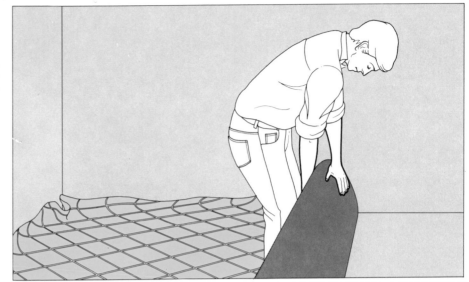

2 **Making relief cuts at corners.** Where the vinyl overlaps an inside corner, cut diagonally across the corner of the sheet, paring away a little at a time until the vinyl fits snugly into the base of the corner *(right)*. At outside corners *(far right)*, cut straight down from the edge of the overlapping vinyl to the base of the corner. At doorframes, make a series of cuts at all internal and external angles straight down from the edge of the vinyl to the base of the frame.

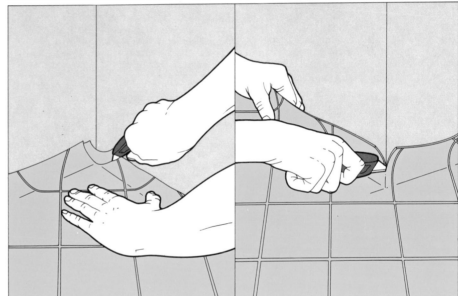

3 **Making a seam.** If a second vinyl sheet is required to cover the floor, measure the distance from the edge of the sheet to the wall and add 100 mm for trimming allowance plus the width of the pattern repeat. Cut the second vinyl sheet roughly to this total width and roll it out. Pull the second sheet over the first until the pattern matches exactly. To protect the knife blade, place an offcut strip of vinyl underneath the sheet edges. Using a metal straightedge to guide the knife, cut straight down through both sheets of vinyl just inside the edge of the overlapping sheet to make neat mating edges. Wherever possible, cut along a straight line in the vinyl pattern. Remove the surplus vinyl and the offcut.

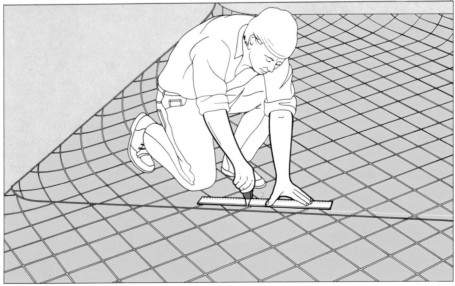

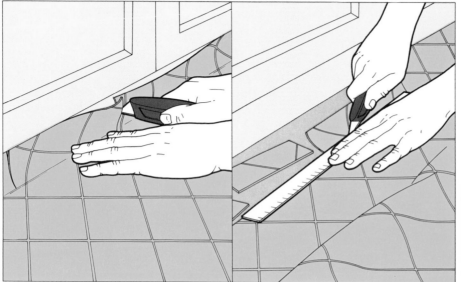

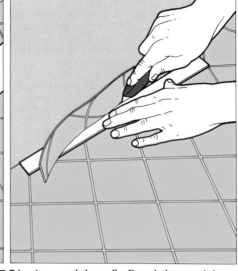

4 **Fitting into toespaces.** Holding the vinyl edge in one hand and the knife in the other, trim back the vinyl overlap all round the walls to about 20 mm. At the toespaces in front of cabinets, make a series of cuts at intervals of about 150 mm straight down from the vinyl edge to the floor *(above, left)*. Pull the cut vinyl away from the toespace; use a straightedge to join up the ends of the cuts and trim off the excess vinyl *(above, right)*.

5 **Trimming round the walls.** Round the remaining roughly trimmed edges of vinyl, use a 150 by 20 by 20 mm strip of wood to force the vinyl into the angle between wall and floor. Remove the wood. For the final trim, hold a metal straightedge as close as possible to the wall, and draw the knife along the edge of the straightedge *(above)*.

Finally, stick down the vinyl flooring with either double-sided adhesive tape *(page 16, Step 6)* or adhesive *(opposite)*.

Fitting Vinyl Round a Central Island

1 **Cutting round the first side.** Central islands can present special problems in fitting; the simplest solution is to use two widths of vinyl and join the seam before final trimming. Plan to position the seam between the sheets as close as possible to the centre of the island. Roll out the first sheet until you reach the island, then unroll the sheet backwards towards the starting wall. Push the rolled-out section of the sheet against the base of the island and, about 100 mm above the floor, cut the sheet from its outside edge towards the centre. Stop the cut about 100 mm short of the edge of the island, then cut back towards the starting wall, stopping the cut about 100 mm short of the depth of the island. Make the first external corner relief cut *(page 17, Step 2)*.

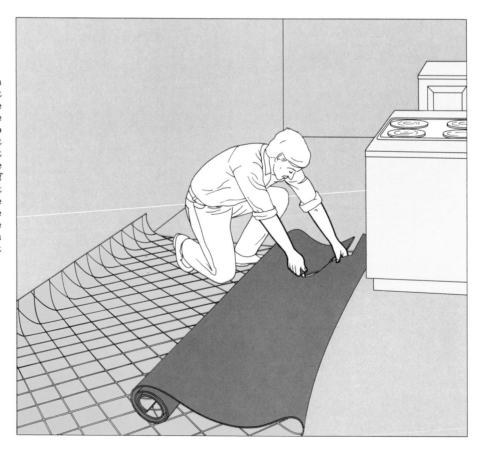

2 **Cutting round the second side.** Lift the roll over the island and lower it to the floor on the other side. Holding the corner of the flap you have made in the sheet, make a relief cut for the second external corner. The surplus material can now be removed by cutting across, parallel to the side of the island and about 100 mm above the floor, to the edge of the sheet.

Roll out the rest of the sheet, then roll out and cut the second sheet in the same way. Make the seam between the sheets as described on page 17, Step 3, and then trim round the island as described in Step 4, opposite.

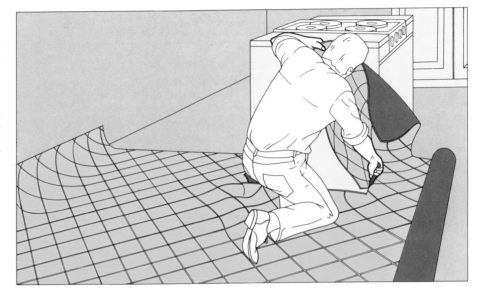

Securing with Adhesive

1 **Applying adhesive.** When bonding a whole sheet of vinyl, roll it half way back on itself to expose the subfloor. Apply the adhesive with a notched trowel, then leave it for the recommended "open time". Lift the edge of the rolled-back vinyl high above the floor and slowly walk it back into place over the adhesive *(right)*. Using an ordinary rolling pin and starting from the centre, carefully roll the vinyl towards each of its edges, taking care to flatten any bulges or air bubbles. Repeat the process for the other half of the vinyl sheet.

If bonding the vinyl perimeter only, roll back each edge in turn and apply a 100 mm-wide band of adhesive to the subfloor. Always follow the adhesive manufacturer's instructions regarding priming, the specifications of the notched trowel to apply the adhesive with, and the length of time for which it must be left exposed to dry.

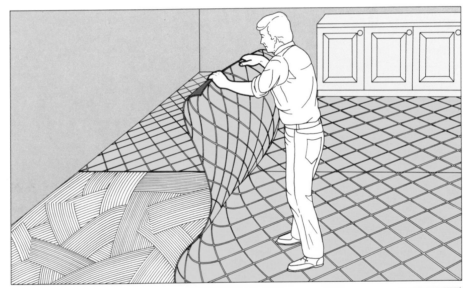

2 **Sealing the seam.** Press the seam together with the thumb and fingers of one hand while applying seam sealer with the other hand. Most seam sealers are applied with a T-shaped nozzle *(inset)* with the top of the T riding on top of the material and the bottom inside the seam. Caution: some manufacturers require that sealing be applied beneath the seam—consult the manufacturer's directions for sealing before carrying out Step 1, above. For either method, wipe away all excess sealing immediately and do not step on the seam for 24 hours after sealing it.

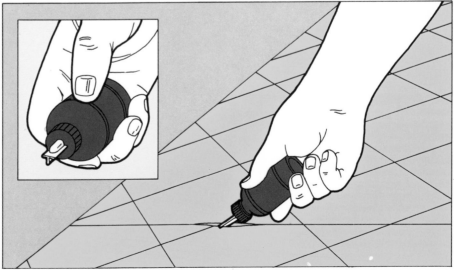

A Moulding Curved for Cleaning

Vinyl cove moulding, shaped as a single concave strip so that it is easy to clean and moisture-resistant, provides a simple alternative to the traditional timber skirting for edging rolled flooring. Two types can be obtained: set-in moulding, which has a square-cut bottom edge and must be installed before the floor covering is laid, and sit-on moulding, which rests on top of the floor covering as shown below. Both types of moulding are available to order from large DIY suppliers in 100 and 75 mm widths. Use special pre-moulded pieces at corners, or scribe and cut the standard lengths to make a neat joint.

Installation is simple, but you must take special precautions with the adhesive, which is noxious and highly inflammable. Turn off all electrical appliances and the pilot lights of any gas cooker before beginning the job; do not smoke; be sure that all windows and doors are wide open; and keep the can of adhesive covered as much as possible, transferring small quantities of the adhesive, as needed, from the can to a piece of scrap plywood.

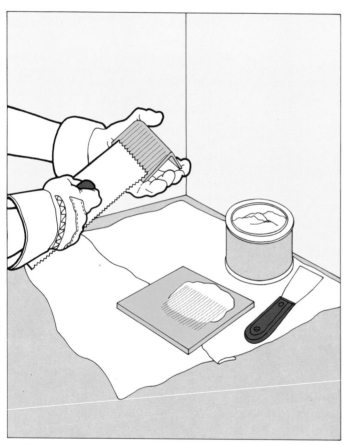

Installing a corner piece. Cover the floor with dustsheets or some old newspapers, then begin the installation at an inside corner. Using a notched trowel, apply vinyl adhesive evenly to the wide vertical surface of an inside corner piece; the short curved edge that rests on the floor need not be glued. Caution: this adhesive is harmful; follow the safety instructions in the text above. Fit the piece carefully into the corner. The adhesive will hold the corner piece almost immediately and will set in about 10 minutes. Remove excess adhesive from the wall with a rag soaked in soap and water.

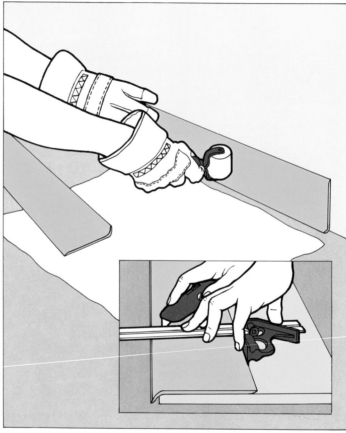

Installing the straight sections. Apply adhesive to the vertical side of a straight 1 metre section of cove and lay the section along the longest wall adjoining the corner piece. Butt it carefully, then press it against the wall with a steel hand roller *(above)* available from your flooring supplier. Add straight sections until you are within 1 metre of the end of the wall. Install the next corner piece and measure a straight length to fill the gap, plus 3 mm to ensure a tight fit. To cut this length, true a combination square against the top edge of the cove and make repeated cuts along it with a trimming knife *(inset)*.

Thresholds to Mate Materials

The last step in installing a kitchen or bathroom floor is to cover the seams in doorways where the edge of the new flooring material meets the adjoining surface. To protect the raised edge of ceramic tile flooring, hardwood thresholds *(below)* make an attractive line and are simple to install. Hard-wearing thresholds made of marble, slate or stone are suitable for doorways where traffic is especially heavy, but these materials must be cut and finished with special equipment by a stonemason.

The width of a threshold depends on whether you wish it to be visible on both sides of the door. If the threshold extends the whole width of the doorjambs, or if it is installed at the side on which the door opens, you may have to plane the bottom of the door to allow it to clear the threshold.

The simplest type of threshold for rolled vinyl or linoleum is a metal edging strip. The metal edging shown here *(bottom)* is shaped to protect a raised edge of vinyl or linoleum; carpet edging *(inset, bottom)* has a narrow slot into which the carpeting can be tucked and secured. Other designs of metal edging are available to cover seams between matching materials.

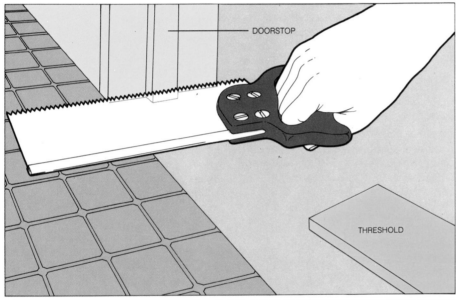

DOORSTOP

THRESHOLD

Installing a threshold. Place the threshold sized to fit between the doorjambs, on the old floor surface and mark its height on the doorstops. Using a tenon saw, cut the doorstops at the marks. Use a wood chisel, if necessary, to remove the pieces of wood. Spread contact adhesive between the doorjambs and along the bottom of the threshold; for a marble, stone or slate threshold, use tile adhesive. Fit the threshold under the trimmed doorstops until it is butted against the floor tiles. Clean off the excess adhesive and allow the threshold to set for at least three hours before grouting between tiles and the threshold.

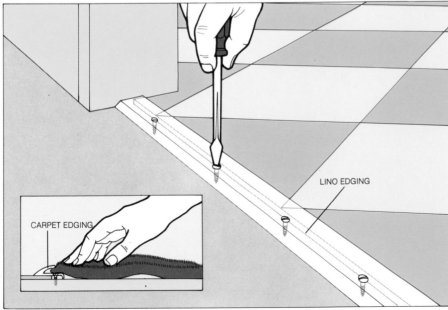

LINO EDGING

CARPET EDGING

Fitting metal edging. Cut the edging with a hacksaw to fit the opening. Place it directly over the seam between the two flooring materials and screw it to the subfloor. When fitting metal edging over a concrete subfloor, drill holes with a masonry drill bit and plug them; drill holes in the same way through ceramic tiles. Carpet edging *(inset)* is screwed to the subfloor so that carpeting can be tucked snugly into the slotted side while the other side covers the edge of the vinyl floor.

Ceramic Tile: Impervious and Permanent

Ceramic tiles of tough fired clay make a durable, beautiful, impervious surface for walls, floors or worktops. Matt, semi-matt or gloss finishes are available, and tiles for floors in particular come in a wide range of surface textures, some of them non-slip.

Plain tiles are produced to match the standard colours of kitchen and bathroom fittings. Patterned tiles may show either a complete pattern on each tile or one quarter of a motif which is completed when four tiles are fixed. Border tiles can be used to frame areas of tiling in contrasting or complementary colours.

Tiles are usually square or rectangular, in sizes ranging from 25 to 300 mm, but other shapes are available. Tiling kits for worktops contain specially shaped edging tiles that prevent water running off the front edge. For easy installation, small tiles called mosaic tiles are sold attached to sheets of paper or a mesh backing. A dealer will tell you how much tile you need if you take him a sketch showing the shape and dimensions of the area to be covered.

Traditional round-edge tiles for setting along exposed edges and at external corners have been largely replaced by glazed-edge tiles, on which the surface glaze runs over on to two of the square sides. Some wall tiles have spacer lugs—small projections on each side—to make equal jointing between the tiles easy. When laying tiles without spacer lugs, use plastic spacers, which are available from tile suppliers, matchsticks, or small pieces of cardboard.

Before ceramic tiles are fixed in place, you must first prepare a smooth surface *(page 8)* and plan a pattern for laying. On floors, rows of dry tiles are laid across the room and adjusted to provide an even border round the perimeter. Timber subfloors or underlayment should be treated with a polyvinyl sealant 24 hours before tiles are laid. Because wall surfaces are often uneven and corners not regular, tiling a wall begins with securing timber battens to provide true vertical and horizontal guidelines for the rows of tiles. On worktops, lay a row of dry tiles along the front of the worktop and adjust as necessary so that the borders at each end are of equal width.

When buying adhesive, consult a dealer and read the label on the container to make sure the product fits your needs as to bonding ability, setting time and water resistance. Most tile adhesives will bond tile to most other surfaces, but there are exceptions; to lay ceramic tile directly over vinyl floor tile, for instance, you need an epoxy adhesive. Adhesives for wall tiling are pre-mixed to a smooth, creamy consistency and come in resealable tubs. Adhesives for floor tiling are cement-based powders which are sold in sealed, polythene-lined bags; water is added to the powder in specified amounts to give a smooth consistency. Rapid-setting adhesives for floor tiling will allow light traffic on the finished floor after 24 hours.

After tiles have been set they must be left until the adhesive has dried; the necessary drying time is specified by the adhesive manufacturer. The joints between the tiles are then filled with grout—a decorative mortar available in a wide range of colours—which seals the joints against dirt and water. Special waterproof grouts are available for tiled areas in kitchens and bathrooms. The grouting powder is mixed with water and rubbed into the joints; after excess grout has been wiped off and the joints have dried, the tiles are polished clean with a soft cloth.

Only simple tools are required—a spirit level and chalk line for laying out tilework, a square for keeping it straight and lastly a notched trowel for spreading adhesive. Buy a trowel that has notches the size and spacing specified on the label of the adhesive container. For cutting the unglazed tiles called quarry tiles, hire a heavy-duty tile cutter such as professionals use. For glazed tiles you can use a carbide-tipped or diamond-tipped tile cutter for scoring straight cuts, and for cutting curves and angles get a pair of nippers, a cutting tool similar to pliers that nibbles away tiles a bit at a time. A carbide-tipped hole saw can save you time and work in making large numbers of round holes and a carbide blade fitted into a hacksaw frame eases the task of cutting out complicated shapes. Protect your eyes with goggles when using nippers, a hole saw or a carbide blade.

The Tricks of Cutting

Making a straight cut. On a tile that has been measured and marked to fit a straight border, score along the pencil line with a tile cutter, using a straightedge as a guide. Place the tile over a pencil, lining up the pencil with the scored line on the tile *(right)*. Press gently on both sides of the tile until it breaks. If the tile is scored too close to the edge to break easily, use tile nippers.

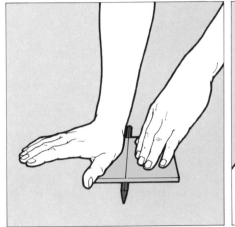

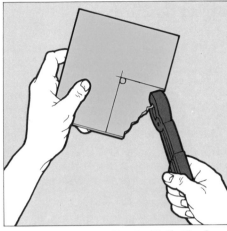

Cutting tiles for corners. To cut a tile that has been marked to fit round a corner, first drill a hole at the point where the marked lines meet, using a carbide-tipped drill bit. Score the marked lines with a tile cutter, then, holding the tile glazed side up, use nippers to nibble away the unwanted part of the tile *(above)*. Take tiny bites—less than 3 mm at a time—to avoid breaking the tile. Smooth the rough-cut edges with an abrasive stone or a file.

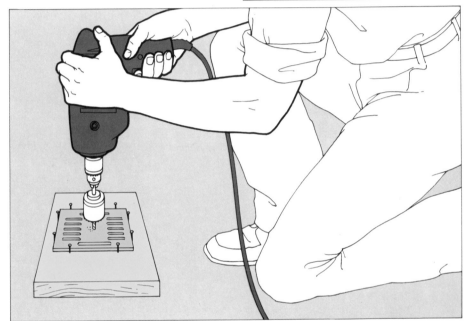

Cutting holes. To cut a hole with a carbide-tipped hole saw, fasten the tile, glazed side down, to a flat piece of wood by driving nails part way in on each side *(left)*. Cut slowly, using firm but not heavy pressure. To fit the tile round a pipe you cannot remove, cut the tile in two through the middle of the hole. To cut a hole with nippers, outline the hole on the face of the tile, cut the tile through the centre of the outline and use the nippers to nibble out the marked area. When the pieces are installed, only a hairline will show between them.

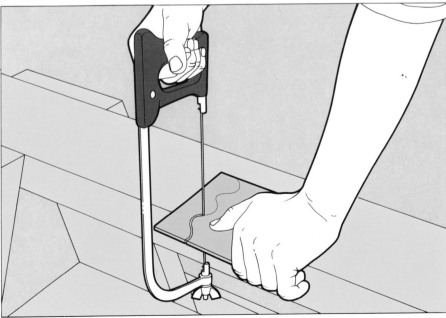

Making a curved cut. Where intricate contours or awkward shapes must be cut, use a round carbide blade fitted into a hacksaw frame to cut along the line. Support the tile firmly with its glazed face upwards and saw carefully through the tile *(right)*. To cut a tile marked with a simple curve, score a line, chip away the excess area with tile nippers, then smooth the edge.

Laying Floor Tiles

1 **Planning a pattern for a floor.** Lay a row of dry tiles from the middle of a doorway to the opposite wall, guided by a string nailed from the centre of the doorway to the wall. If a gap of less than half a tile width remains at the end of the run, remove the first tile and centre the remaining tiles. The resulting spaces left for the two border tiles will equal more than half the width of a tile, avoiding awkward cuts on tiny pieces. Lay a second row of dry tiles at right angles to the first row at the end opposite the doorway. If necessary, remove a tile and centre the row to allow for border tiles at least half a tile wide, then slide the first row over so that the two rows intersect *(right)*. As a guide for laying the tiles, snap intersecting chalk lines along both rows, then snap a third chalk line at right angles to the last tile in the corner farthest from the doorway.

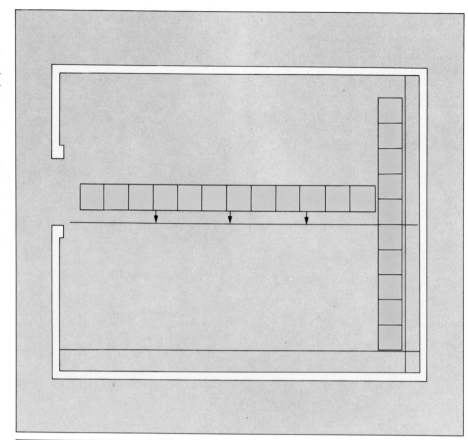

2 **Applying adhesive.** Start applying adhesive at the corner of the room farthest away from the doorway. Do not apply adhesive round the edge of the room for border tiles: these will be cut and set after all the uncut tiles have been laid. Use a notched trowel with its edge held at an angle of 45 degrees to the floor surface to spread adhesive over an area of about 1 square metre. Use only about a cup of adhesive at a time so that the adhesive flows freely from the notches. Avoid covering the chalk lines.

3 **Setting tiles.** Set the first tiles in the corner where you have started to apply adhesive, using the chalk lines as guides. Press each tile in place with your fingertips, twisting it slightly to set it into the adhesive; do not slide tiles into place or adhesive will fill the grout joint and make grouting impossible. When setting thick tiles with indentations on the backs, apply adhesive also to the back of each tile.

Keep the spaces for grouting between tiles regular; if necessary, insert spacers or matchsticks between the tiles as you lay them.

4 **Beating in the tile.** Pad a piece of wood the length of three tiles with several layers of cloth. When you finish laying tiles on each area prepared with adhesive, put the beater, padded side down, on the set tiles and tap it gently with a hammer several times along its length. Beating in sets the tiles more firmly into the adhesive and helps to ensure a level floor.

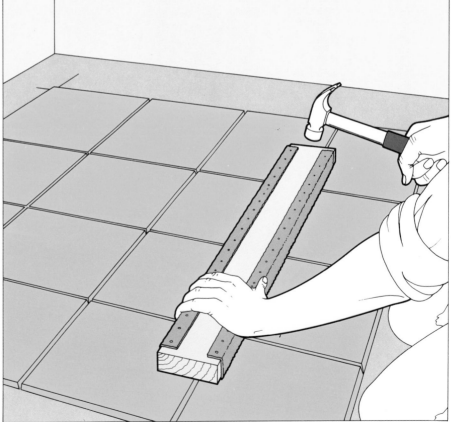

5 **Marking border tiles.** Measure and cut the border tiles individually when you have completed laying all the uncut tiles. To mark a straight border tile, place a dry tile face-up on top of the last fixed tile, then butt a second tile on top of this against the wall; using the edge of the second tile as a guide, mark across the face of the first dry tile with a tile cutter or pencil *(right)*.

For border tiles abutting curved edges, such as those of a W.C. or a basin pedestal, trace the uncovered area on to paper and use this as a template to mark the tile.

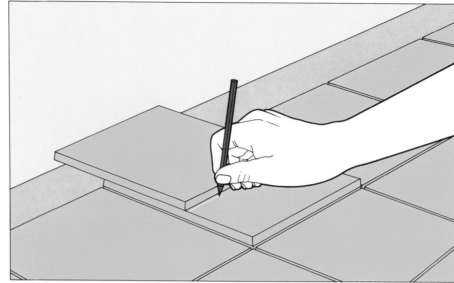

6 **Marking corner tiles.** Place a dry tile face-up over the last fixed tile parallel to one side of the corner, then butt another tile against the wall on top of this and mark along its edge on the tile beneath. Move the marked tile—without turning it—on to the last fixed tile on the other side of the corner, butt the second tile against the wall and mark again along its edge *(right)*.

To allow space for grouting, cut all border and corner tiles about 3 mm inside the marked lines, using the appropriate cutting techniques as described on page 23. When all the tiles have been cut, smoothed and laid dry in position, apply adhesive to the floor surface and affix them. Let the adhesive set for 24 hours before grouting.

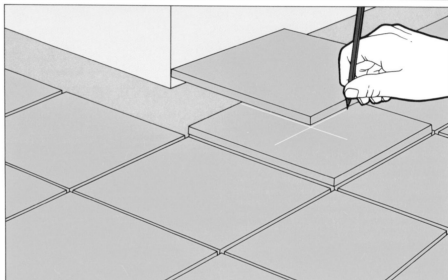

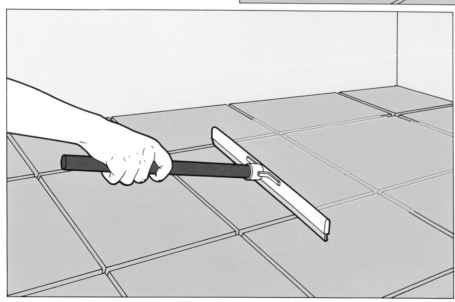

7 **Grouting.** Mix grout to the consistency specified by the manufacturer. Spread it across the floor with a window-washing squeegee or stiff cardboard, forcing it into the joints between tiles. Wipe off excess grout with a damp sponge or cloth, rinsing the sponge or cloth frequently. When all grout has been removed, let the tiles dry; polish with a soft cloth.

Setting Sheets of Tile

Mosaic tile sheets. Most mosaic tiles come in sheets held together by paper on the face of the tiles or by mesh on the back. Roll up the sheet with the back of the tiles outside. After trowelling on adhesive, place the free edge of the sheet where it is to be set and gradually unroll the sheet, pressing the tiles gently into the adhesive. Do not slide sheets into place. Space sheets the same distance apart as the tiles in the sheets. The mesh on mesh-mounted tiles remains in place under the tiles; the paper on paper-faced tiles is removed after the tiles are set by dampening it and peeling it off.

When mosaic tiles must be cut to fit a space, cut the affected tiles out of the sheet, trim them as necessary and set them individually.

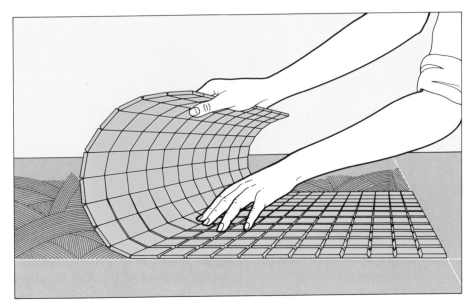

Setting Tiles in a Wall

POSITION OF FIRST TILE

1 Fixing the starting point. To determine the position of the first tile to be set, make a gauge lathe by marking tile widths—and the spaces for grouting between them—along a length of wood. Use the lathe to find out how many uncut tiles will fit along the wall, then move the lathe to allow for border tiles of equal size at each end and mark its left-hand end on the wall. Whenever possible, allow for equal-sized border tiles

round windows also. For ease of cutting, border tiles should be half to three quarters of the width of a full tile.

If you are tiling the whole wall, use the lathe gauge in the same way to allow for equal-sized border tiles at top and bottom; if tiling only part way up the wall, use the lathe to find out how many uncut tiles will fit from the finished height to floor level, and mark its bottom edge.

Position a 30 by 15 mm length of wood along the bottom of the wall with its top edge aligned with the mark for the lowest uncut tile. Use a spirit level to check that the batten is horizontal, then temporarily fasten it to the wall with nails or screws. Fasten a second 30 by 15 mm batten up the left-hand side of the wall, aligning it with the mark for the first uncut tile. Check that the batten is vertical with a spirit level or plumbline.

2 **Setting the tiles.** Starting at the right-angled corner formed by the vertical and horizontal battens, spread tile adhesive using a trowel or float to a thickness of 3 to 5 mm over an area of one square metre. Comb the adhesive with a notched trowel or spreader to leave horizontal ridges *(below)*. Beginning along the bottom row, press the tiles into place with a slight twisting action. If the tiles have no spacer lugs, use plastic spacers or matchsticks to ensure equal spacing between the tiles. After covering each square metre of adhesive, check the vertical and horizontal alignment of the tiles with a spirit level.

3 **Finishing the wall.** Complete the fixing of all whole tiles on the wall, then mark and cut tiles for borders round window frames and other fixtures as described on page 26, Steps 5 and 6. If you are not tiling up to the ceiling, use glazed-edge tiles along the top row. At window ledges, use full-size glazed-edge tiles to cover the top edges of vertical tiles *(below)*; cut border tiles for the back, not the front of the ledges. Leave the tiles to set for 12 hours, then remove the timber battens and set border tiles along the bottom of the wall and up the starting side. Wait 24 hours before grouting *(page 26, Step 7)*.

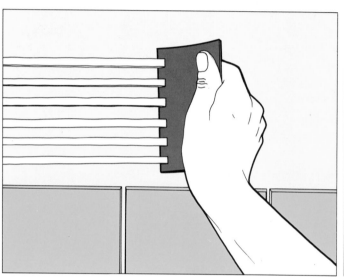

Making Minor Repairs

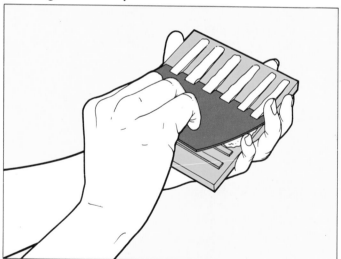

Patching small areas. To replace broken tiles or reset loose tiles, remove tiles from the damaged area with a hammer and cold chisel, then apply the adhesive and set the tiles as on page 25. If cramped working space makes applying adhesive to the surface difficult, spread it on the backs of the tiles. If replacement tiles or tiles being reset do not have built-in spacer lugs, space the tiles with plastic spacers or matchsticks.

Repairing grout lines. Use an awl to pick out damaged or discoloured grout. Mix a little grout, matching the old colour as closely as possible, and wipe it into the joint with your finger. A pencil eraser or the butt end of an old toothbrush may be helpful in forcing grout into the joint. Pack the joint tightly, then wipe away any excess and polish the tiles.

Accessories for Bathroom Walls

The essential bathroom accessories—soap dishes, towel rails and toilet roll holders—and many less essential ones are available in three types. Flush-set accessories mount on the wall much like tile or panelling; they are installed at the time the wall covering is applied. Recessed accessories, the least common type, are fitted into holes in the wall at the same stage of wall finishing. The third type, surface-mounted accessories, can be installed at any time over the wall covering; some are merely glued on, but the ones held by screws and mounting clips are usually sturdier. The method of fastening the accessory to the clip depends on whether the accessory is ceramic or metal (right).

When screwing surface-mounted accessories to a solid wall, ensure that the wall plugs are recessed behind the tile covering. This precaution prevents tiles from cracking when the plugs expand as screws are tightened. On timber-frame walls, screw directly into a stud wherever possible; if studs are not located conveniently, use hollow-wall fixings.

Vertical or L-shaped grab bars, which resemble towel rails but are more sturdily mounted, are a useful addition to any bathroom for the elderly. Like other surface-mounted accessories, they are fixed on top of the wall covering.

If a wall is being tiled, flush-set accessories are generally installed. Leave an opening for them at the time of tiling, cutting tiles as needed to trim the edges of the space. When setting or replacing a flush-set accessory, apply tile adhesive to the back of the accessory as you would when replacing a broken tile (opposite, below).

Recessed accessories can be installed in any solid wall that can be cut, and are suitable for tiled walls if a space for them is planned and the underlaying material is cut before tiling. The small opening in the wall must be cut to the same dimensions as the accessory's recessed part.

Surface-Mounted Pieces

Drilling tile. Locate accessories with screw holes as near to the centres of tiles as possible. Use masking tape to stick a piece of thin card where the accessory is to be fastened. Hold the mounting clip for the accessory against the card and mark the screw holes (below). Drill with a masonry bit and a variable-speed drill at low speed; apply light pressure to avoid breaking the tile. After the holes are drilled, peel the card from the wall.

Installing ceramic accessories. Screw the metal mounting clip into plastic wall plugs, ensuring that it is secured the correct way up. Slide the accessory down over the wedge-shaped clip until it fits snugly against the wall.

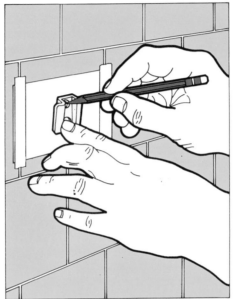

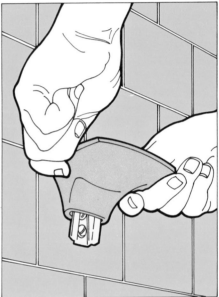

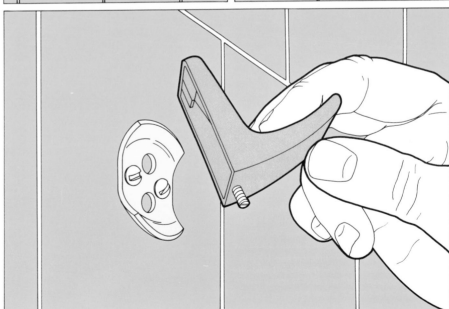

Installing metal accessories. Attach the clip to the wall as shown above, with its angled parts at top and bottom. Place the set-screw in the bottom of the accessory. Slip the top of the accessory over the top angle of the mounting clip and drop the bottom of the accessory over the bottom of the clip. Tighten the set-screw against the bottom of the clip with a small screwdriver.

Plastic Laminates: Easy to Mount and Maintain

Plastic laminate—the tough, impermeable, stain-resistant material that is now almost universal for kitchen worktops—also makes attractive covering for tables, vanity units, cabinet doors and even walls. Prelaminated worktops, cabinets and other kitchen and bathroom fittings are readily available, but if you are constructing your own fittings from scratch in order, for example, to ensure a perfect fit along irregular walls, you will have to finish their exposed surfaces yourself. Applying laminate sheets is almost as easy as painting and generally far more satisfactory for surfaces subject to heavy wear.

Most laminates used on surfaces other than walls come in sheets 1.5 mm thick; walls *(pages 33–35)* require a different thickness. The sheets expand and contract with changes in temperature and humidity and should be allowed to adapt to the room where they will be used—stack them loosely against a wall for 48 hours before cutting them.

Laminates can be applied over plywood, chipboard, hardboard or old laminate, but it is almost impossible to apply them over ceramic tiles or linoleum; such surfaces must first be covered with underlayment to which the laminate is then bonded.

Contact adhesives for bonding laminate sheets contain a highly inflammable and toxic solvent. Special thixotropic adhesives allow the laminate to be laid and then manoeuvred into exact alignment before the adhesive hardens. Because of the hazards of solvent-based adhesives—and because of the difficulty of handling large sheets of laminate in small rooms—work outdoors as much as possible. Moderate temperatures are necessary; contact adhesives dry tediously slowly at temperatures much below 20°C and at higher temperatures they dry too fast and lose their bonding strength. If you must work indoors, keep the adhesive away from heat, sparks and any open flames. Do not smoke while working, extinguish pilot lights and gas burners, and switch off cookers, heaters and other electric appliances. Make sure you provide cross-ventilation in the work area, and avoid inhaling adhesive fumes.

Applying laminate to worktops or similar surfaces is easiest when the worktop is being built *(pages 38–41)* or when it has been removed to a roomy work area. If removing an already installed worktop is not practical, remove the sink or any other fixtures recessed into cutouts, then apply laminate with the worktop in place *(page 38)*. All cutouts in new laminate are made after the laminate has been bonded.

As contact adhesive dries, it causes the core material to contract slightly on the side that has been treated. To prevent cabinet doors and other components that are not permanently fixed from becoming bowed, apply laminate to both back and front surfaces. For the back surfaces, a thinner, cheaper laminate can be used.

Any surface to be laminated should be clean, dry and even, with any protrusions sanded down and holes filled with wood filler. If you apply new laminate directly over the old, flatten bubbles by breaking them with a hammer and sanding them down, or by countersinking a flat-head wood screw through the bubble into the base. Re-bond loose edges and sand the whole surface thoroughly before applying adhesive; sand, sawdust or laminate chips left on the worktop will make permanent lumps in the finished surface.

The edges of a laminate-covered worktop can be finished in a number of ways *(page 32, below)*. The inside joint between the worktop and the wall can be sealed with a flexible plastic moulding, while hardwood moulding provides an attractive alternative to laminate edging strips.

Covering a Worktop

1 Cutting laminate. Mark the pieces to be cut out of each laminate sheet 5 mm larger in all dimensions than the surfaces to be covered, to provide a margin for trimming. When laminating a worktop that has been removed from the base units, plan to remove the splashback and cover the whole top surface *(Step 2, opposite)*. For a worktop being laminated in place with the splashback attached, cover the top surface up to the bottom edge of the splashback.

Place the marked sheet face up on a firm support or on the floor, and score the sheet with a laminate scriber or with a laminate blade in an ordinary trimming knife. Then bend the edge of the sheet upwards *(right)* until it snaps along the scored line. You can also cut the sheet with a jigsaw using a fine-toothed blade, but test the blade on a scrap of laminate first to make sure it will not cause excessive chipping.

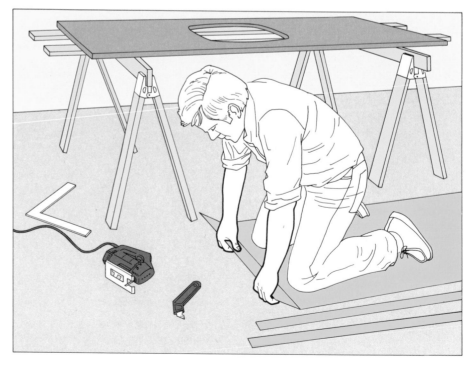

2 **Bonding a top surface.** Apply adhesive to the top surface and the laminate back with a serrated spreader, using a little extra adhesive round the edges of both. When the adhesive is dry, lay strips of wood 20 mm thick at 300 mm intervals across the top surface. Lay the laminate face up on the wood supports and aligned with the top surface. Slide out one end support and press that end of the laminate sheet down. Remove remaining supports one at a time, pressing down the laminate as you work towards the other end of the surface. To ensure a firm bond, tap the whole surface with a wood block and hammer.

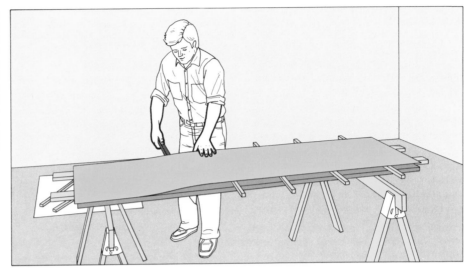

3 **Trimming projections.** Use a block plane to trim the excess laminate flush with the worktop sides *(right)*. Work from the edges towards the centre of each side to prevent chipping at the corners. Trimming can also be performed with a special laminate trimmer or with a router; if you use the latter, you should wear goggles to protect your eyes from flying particles.

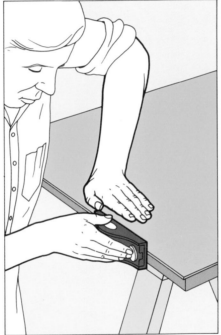

4 **Putting on edge strips.** Attach edge strips first at the short sides of the worktop. If you are laminating a U-shaped worktop, begin at the bottom of the U. If you plan to use hardwood moulding, see instructions on page 32.

    Apply adhesive to both laminate and edge. When the adhesive has dried, hold an edge strip between thumbs and forefingers *(below)*; position it as accurately as possible and set it in place. Tap the surface with a hammer and wood block. Trim off the projecting laminate as in Step 3, above, then bevel the sharp edges along the top and at corners with a block plane held at a 45-degree angle. To bend laminate round a gentle curve, soak it in hot water until it becomes flexible, wipe it dry and attach it before it cools.

5 **Making cutouts.** Cut out holes for sinks, plumbing and electrical outlets after attaching laminate. If you are relaminating an old surface that already has cutouts, drill a 25 mm hole inside the line of each cutout and cut the laminate with a router, following the rim of the original hole. If you have made an entirely new worktop, mark each cutout as shown on page 40, Step 6. Drill a 6 mm starter hole—and a hole at each corner for cutouts with corners—and cut the opening using a jigsaw fitted with a metal-cutting blade.

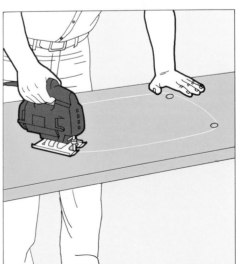

Edging a Splashback in Place

Covering the splashback. When laminating the splashback of a worktop that has not been detached from the base units, apply laminate first to the front of the splashback and trim the top edge flush with a sanding block. Apply a strip cut as accurately as possible to the top edge of the splashback *(right)* and bevel the sharp edges with the sanding block held at a 45-degree angle.

If you are covering a worktop detached from the base units, cover the splashback as you did the other surfaces—bonding first the front, then the ends and finally the top. Reattach the splashback after lamination as on pages 41–42, Steps 8–9; put a bead of silicone seal along the bottom edge of the splashback to waterproof the joint.

With the worktop in place, caulk between the top edge of the splashback and the wall as necessary. If there is no splashback, seal the wall edges of the worktop as shown below, right.

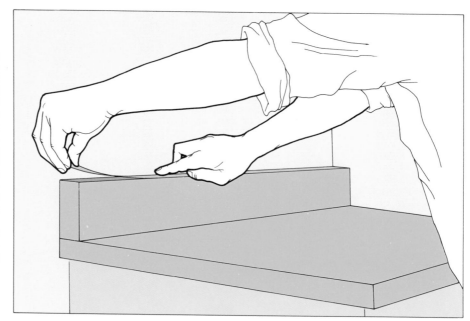

Finishing Edges with Moulding

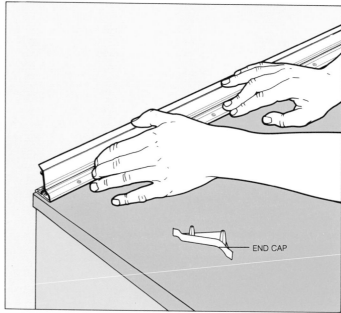

END CAP

Adding a hardwood edge. Measure the exposed sides of the worktop; at each external corner, add the thickness of the hardwood moulding to allow for the mitred joints. Cut the moulding using a tenon saw and mitre box, making 45-degree cuts for the corners. Apply contact adhesive to both the worktop edges and the inside faces of the moulding, then press the glued surfaces together. Wipe off any excess glue with a rag and contact adhesive thinners. If the moulding is slightly wider than the thickness of the laminated worktop, use a block plane to trim the moulding flush with the worktop edges. The hardwood can then be finished with teak oil or polyurethane varnish, applied with a brush or soft cloth.

Sealing inside edges. Plastic moulding for covering the gap between worktops and walls consists of a slotted base strip, a covering strip shaped to protect the worktop edge and deflect water, and a range of corner joints and end caps. To install the moulding, subtract from the worktop dimensions the widths of the appropriate corner and end fittings, and cut the strips to length. Press the base strip against the wall along the inside edge of the worktop and mark through the screwholes with a pencil. Remove the base strip, drill pilot holes in the worktop, and secure the base strip with 12 mm No. 4 twinfast chipboard screws. Press the covering strip into the slot in the base strip, and fit the external corner joints and end caps where necessary. Internal corner joints must be slotted into the covering strips before they are pressed into the base strip.

Panelling Walls

Plastic laminate which is used for walls comes factory-bonded to an underlayment of hardboard, chipboard or plywood. The panels are 3 to 5 mm thick and they come in sheets up to 2440 by 1220 mm.

Laminate panels can be mounted on almost any flat, clean surface, including plastic, wallboard or tile. Wallpaper or vinyl wall covering should be removed, however, and painted surfaces will need to be scraped and sanded. Repair any cracks or holes in plaster-faced walls *(page 9)* and check that walls are even by sliding a long, straight-edged board across the wall surface, looking for gaps between board and wall. If the walls are uneven, install a framework of battens with shims to provide a level backing for the panels *(right)*.

Leave the laminate panels for 24 hours to adjust to the room temperature, then cut the panels as for worktops *(pages 30–32)*. Joints between panels are sealed with metal or vinyl mouldings *(right, below)*, into which the edges of panels fit. If necessary, bevel the panel edge along the back to let it fit easily. Never nail into the panel.

Wherever the horizontal moulding meets the vertical moulding, as when installing wainscoting *(page 34)*, you should trim or mitre the ends of moulding strips to make a smooth fit.

Trim and fit each panel carefully before applying adhesive to the wall and the panel; you will usually have only a tiny margin for error. Make all cutouts for wall fixtures before installing the panels.

Most panel adhesives are highly inflammable. Handle adhesives with the same care as other laminate adhesives *(page 30)*, and keep the room well ventilated. Follow the manufacturer's instructions on adhesive application and drying time. Some panel adhesives bond instantly, requiring great skill in aligning panels; others bond more slowly, allowing time for adjustments. A properly applied adhesive provides a watertight bond between wall and panel, but be sure to apply a silicone seal along the tops and bottoms of panels for complete moisture protection.

A Framework for an Uneven Wall

Making a wall level. A framework of 50 by 25 mm battens attached to a wall will provide an even, plumb backing for panels. First, skirting boards and architraves are removed and replaced by battens, then horizontal battens are spaced at intervals of about 450 mm; the vertical battens are spaced to coincide with the butt joints between panels. The battens are fixed to a masonry wall with screws and wallplugs; on timber frame walls, hollow-wall fixings are used where the battens cannot be screwed directly into studs. Before the screws are tightened check for plumb and insert small wooden wedges—also known as shims—behind each batten to pack out the framework over shallow depressions and other surface irregularities.

Mouldings to Seal the Edges

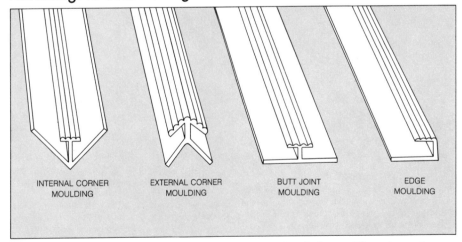

INTERNAL CORNER MOULDING   EXTERNAL CORNER MOULDING   BUTT JOINT MOULDING   EDGE MOULDING

Designs for different joints. Cut from long strips of metal or plastic, mouldings are usually installed a length at a time with the laminate panels *(page 34)*. Shown above are internal and external corner mouldings that accommodate two panels that meet at a corner; butt-joint moulding to cover seams between adjoining panels on the same wall; and edge moulding, also used as cap moulding along the tops of panels in wainscot installations. The corner mouldings illustrated must be fixed to the wall before the panels are installed; mouldings for internal and external corners are also available in strips designed to be attached to finished panels.

Putting Up the Panels

1 Installing moulding. Remove skirting boards, ceiling mouldings and wall fixtures. Secure a corner moulding strip to the wall with contact adhesive; alternatively, countersunk screws may be used on solid walls or, on timber frame walls, nails driven into the studs and then countersunk with a nail punch.

For wainscot installations, draw a horizontal guideline at the desired height on the wall or walls to be panelled. Mount vertical moulding as for full-wall installations. Secure horizontal edge moulding to cap the top edges of panels before the panels are fixed. Where the horizontal edge moulding meets vertical moulding, cut away the flanges of the edge moulding to ensure a smooth fit *(inset)*.

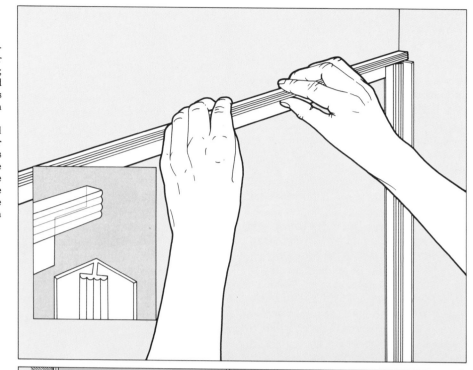

2 Making cutouts. Where cutouts will be required in a panel for a pipe, measure the vertical distance from the centre of the pipe to the floor or ceiling and the horizontal distance to the wall or adjacent panel. Transfer these measurements to the panel, and at the point where they intersect cut a hole of the same diameter as the pipe with a hole saw. Where complex cutouts or contours must be cut, tape stiff paper or card to the wall and make a template, as on pages 14–16.

3 Mounting panels. Place cardboard shims about 3 mm thick on the floor along the wall. Begin panelling in the corner where the moulding is in place. Cut a panel to the required height and fit a strip of butt-joint moulding along its outside edge. Then apply adhesive to the wall and to the back of the panel and moulding with a notched spreader. When the adhesive dries to the consistency recommended by the manufacturer, mount the panel on the wall, sliding its inside edge into the groove of the corner moulding. To ensure firm bonding, apply pressure over the whole surface with a hammer and wood block.

Continue round the room, mounting panels and moulding strips, in the same way as for the first panel, so that you finish at the starting point. When the installation is complete, remove the shims from the panel bottoms and then refix the skirting boards or fasten vinyl cove moulding along the base of the walls.

4 **Door and window treatments.** Mount a strip of edge moulding as close to the door or window architrave as possible and fit one end of the panel into it. To fit panel edges round protruding window sills, make a template and cut the panel to the pattern you have traced.

If you prefer not to use moulding, you can remove the wood architraves of the door or window and, using a router, make grooves 25 mm wide and 3 mm deep along the wall edges. Mount panels so that they will extend into the groove, then remount the door or window architraves over the panel edges.

Finishing Round a Bath

1 **Mounting the panels.** Cut and fit the panels, make cutouts for fixtures, and mount panels in the same manner as other wall installations. To cut an end wall panel to fit precisely the curvature of a bath shoulder, measure and mark on the face of the panel the dimensions of the corner to be cut out. Then bend a piece of wire solder around the curve of the shoulder, transfer this curve to the panel markings by tracing the bent solder *(left)*, and cut out the corner.

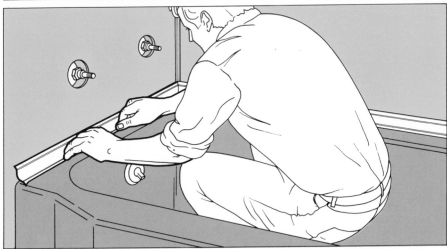

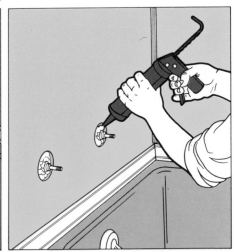

2 **Sealing round the bath.** Plastic L-shaped moulding for sealing round the top of a bath is attached to the wall only, thus allowing a bath to rise and fall slightly without disturbing the fixing. Measure and cut the moulding strip to the length required; at corners, make 45-degree cuts for mitre joints. Attach the moulding with contact adhesive; if the contact adhesive is supplied in one continuous strip, first press it to the back of the moulding, then strip off the release paper and, working outwards from the centre of the strip, press it firmly against the wall panelling and down on to the bath at the same time.

3 **Sealing the cutouts.** Using a caulking gun, squeeze a bead of sealant into the gaps between the cutouts and the panel *(above)*. Wipe off any excess sealant with a damp cloth before reattaching the fixtures.

2 New Fittings for Convenience

Truing a cabinet. The spirit level and shims seen on top of this kitchen cabinet are needed to install it properly. Because floors and walls are seldom exactly flat surfaces, each cabinet must be adjusted with thin wood shim strips to push it forwards or upwards to align it with the others. Only when the cabinets are true—that is, perfectly horizontal and vertical—are they screwed to the walls and to each other *(pages 44–46)*.

Perhaps surprisingly, many important fittings and accessories can be installed in kitchens and bathrooms without having to interfere with the plumbing at all. Using only basic woodworking tools—hammers, saws, drills and the rest—you can add to storage capacity, increase efficiency and improve appearance.

Carpentry in these rooms, however, calls for special care. Both are generally small places, crowded and short of working space, and both are likely to include coverings on walls, floors and worktops that, while resistant to moisture and chemicals, are brittle and easily cracked. You must often create an assembly area outside a room and, when you work inside, protect surfaces with newspapers. The trick is to analyse a job beforehand, separating inside from outside work.

Installing cabinets *(pages 44–47)* is inside work, of course: the units come ready-made, and the jobs of mounting them and linking them into a single braced structure must be done on the walls and floors they occupy. But adding a fitted worktop to a set of base cabinets is something that can be done outside almost entirely. If you do not have a large kitchen like the one shown on pages 38–43, use your workshop, or if necessary the garage or garden, to cut a core for the worktop, assemble it and cover it with tiles or plastic laminate.

Smaller jobs, in which minor changes have the effect of major improvements, make easy inside work—horizontal shelving is replaced by vertical dividers or by drawers mounted on glides, a spare cabinet gets a retractable refuse bin, a swivelling carousel tray provides access to hard-to-reach corners *(pages 48–51)*. Bigger inside jobs will take you into normally hidden areas, and call for more careful preparation. The first stage in the installation of a serving hatch *(pages 56–61)* is to knock out an opening in an inside wall; a fan for bathroom ventilation and an extractor hood for a cooker *(pages 52–55)* both require a smaller hole in an outside wall for ducting. In each case you must cut off electrical circuits in the room and may have to disturb existing plumbing. For jobs such as these, it is best to clear the room of all obstructions and close it off before commencing work.

Improvements in the appearance of a room usually lend themselves well to a combination of inside and outside work. You can, for instance, update an old-fashioned claw-footed bath by boxing it in with water-resistant plywood, and then provide extra storage space by building a cabinet extension on the end of the boxed-in bath *(pages 67–69)*—and for both jobs you can make the big pieces for the assembly outside the bathroom. The most luxurious addition of all is another such job. The steam bath called a sauna *(pages 62–66)* was once as rare—and almost as expensive—as a private swimming pool. Today, a home carpenter with just over one square metre of space can put one together in a weekend—and then relax in steamy splendour.

A Custom-Made Worktop for a Ready-Made Base

The standard kitchen worktop is essentially a long board 30 to 40 mm thick and about 600 mm deep. A vertical splashback 100 mm high is sometimes attached to the top along the rear edge, and the entire assembly rises about 900 mm above the floor. Many modern worktops have self-rimmed sinks and cooking hobs set into them. A flange-like, stainless-steel sink frame may be used to support some sink models and also such inserts as chopping boards and heatproof plates.

A worktop may consist of a solid length of hardwood or of a textured synthetic material. Alternatively, it may also consist of a less expensive material, such as chipboard or exterior-grade plywood, covered with a decorative surface such as ceramic tile or high-pressure laminated plastic. For the installation of plastic laminates and tiles, see pages 22–27 and 30–32. Tiles for worktops are available in special kits.

As an alternative to such an assembly, you can buy a worktop complete with a factory-installed laminate. Such factory-made tops are easy to install—you need only saw them to the correct length, cut out the openings for sinks or other inserts and then screw them to the base units—but, because they come in standard widths, they cannot be fitted precisely to any bowed or bumpy walls. Use a butt joint when fitting two lengths of factory-made worktop in a right-angled corner; if the corner is out of square, cut both lengths of worktop to make a mitre joint, as illustrated on page 43. For butt joints between worktops with rounded front edges, use a special jointing strip.

Constructing your own worktop from scratch offers you two important advantages over a factory-made top: you are able to fit the back of the worktop precisely to the contours of an irregular wall, and you can minimize water seepage by covering joints in the core material with laminate or tiling. Depending on the dimensions of your base units and of your sheet of core material, you may be able to cut an L-shaped worktop core without any joints from a single sheet. To determine the worktop's depth, measure the distance from the cabinet front to the wall and add 50 mm for overhang. The length depends on the layout of the cabinets; set a top over the long leg of an L-shaped layout, and add 50 mm of overhang for ends that do not abut a wall. If the walls are slightly bowed or meet at an angle greater than 90 degrees, you will have to allow for these irregularities when marking out the timber *(below)*, and then scribe and cut the worktop to fit *(Steps 3 and 4)*.

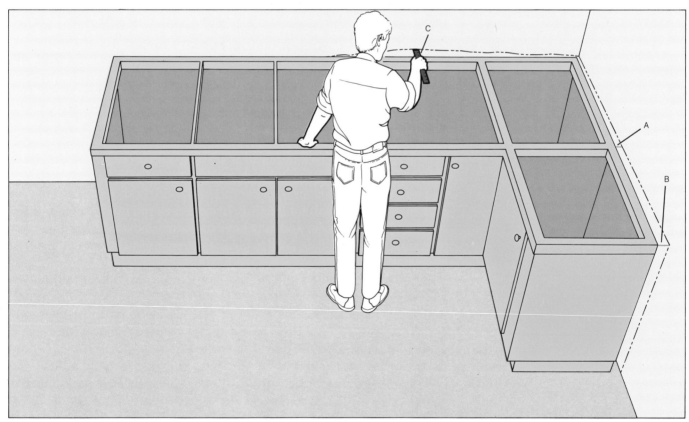

1 Measuring for irregular walls. Measure any gaps between the walls and the ready-made base units at their widest span. In the L-shaped assembly shown here the widest points along the longer leg of the "L" are at C, caused by a bowed wall, and at A, the result of an out of square wall. The widest point along the short leg of the "L" is at point B, also caused by the out of square wall. To establish the dimensions for the longer leg of the worktop, add distance C to the depth and distance A to the length of the longer leg of the base unit, then add 50 mm overhang allowance to each measurement. The length of the shorter leg of the worktop will be the same as the shorter leg of the base unit, but its depth will be equivalent to the width of the base unit, plus the distance B, plus 50 mm overhang allowance.

2 Assembling the core. With a circular saw or jigsaw, cut out two pieces of core 18 mm thick to the right length and depth. To join the pieces at right angles, apply PVA woodworking glue to the edges, then reinforce the joint with corrugated steel fasteners driven across the seam at 40 mm intervals. Turn the board upside down and hammer a second series of corrugated fasteners across the back of the seam.

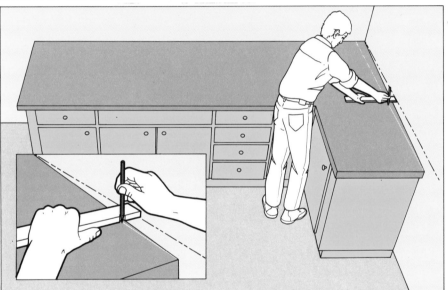

3 Scribing along the angled wall. Place the worktop core on top of the base unit, butted into the corner. Hold one end of an offcut piece of timber against the wall at the end of the short leg of the core, and mark on the timber the width of the gap. Cut a notch in the timber at this point. Holding the point of a pencil in the notch *(inset)*, push the offcut along the wall towards the corner to draw a line along the core that is parallel to the wall *(left)*. Remove the worktop core from the base unit, support it on sawhorses and cut along the pencil line.

4 Scribing along the bowed wall. Replace the core on top of the base unit and push it into the corner. The shorter leg of the core should now be touching the wall along its entire length. To scribe along the long leg of the core, cut a notch in the offcut at the widest gap between the bowed wall and the core, and draw a pencil line parallel to the wall in the same way as described in Step 3. Remove the core from the base unit and cut along the pencil line.

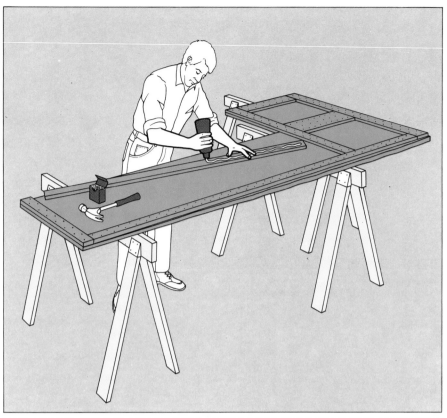

5 **Installing the battens.** To increase the thickness of the core, you must add strips called battens 75 mm wide and 18 mm thick. Cut the battens from stock to match the sides of the core, butting at the corners; the locations of the butt joints are unimportant, but the strips must cover the perimeter of the core. Except along the two sides that have been scribed and cut to fit along the walls, the battens must be installed flush with the outside edges of the core.

Turn the core upside down, apply a ribbon of PVA glue to the wide surface of a batten strip and press the glued batten to the core. Secure the batten with 32 mm oval nails or panel pins, spaced 40 mm apart. Repeat the procedure for all the battens. If the worktop contains a butt joint, cut a batten 150 mm wide to the length of the exposed seam and install it along the joint.

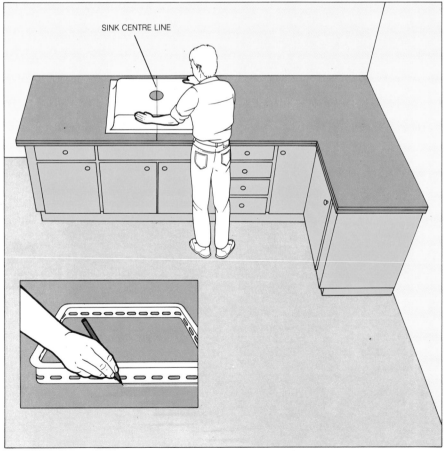

SINK CENTRE LINE

6 **Positioning a sink.** Mark the centre on the front edge of the sink base unit. Set the core on the base units and draw a pencil line across the top of the core from front to rear at the midpoint of the sink base unit. Rest the sink upside down on the core, and mark the midpoints of the front and rear rim. Line up the marks on the rim with the line on the core and move the sink along this line until the rim is at least 75 mm from the front of the core and 25 mm from the rear. Then trace round the sink's rim.

For a sink supported by a stainless steel frame (*inset*), centre the rim upright on the pencil line and trace the outline. Chopping boards and heatproof plate inserts can be sited almost anywhere on the worktop, as long as they are at least 75 mm from the front and 25 mm from the rear.

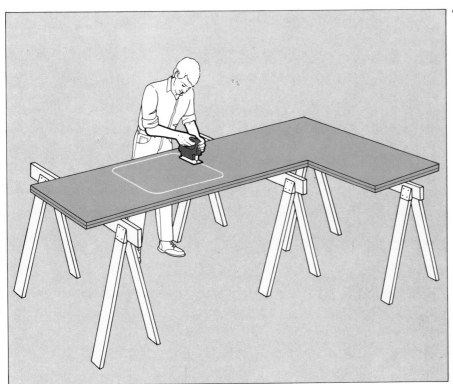

7 **Making the sink cutout.** Set the sink aside and return the core to the sawhorses. Mark points 6 mm inside the outline of the sink rim on all four sides and, using a straightedge and soft pencil, connect the marks to outline a sink cutout 6 mm inside the original. Drill a pilot hole 25 mm inside the outline and, beginning at this hole, cut along the outline with a jigsaw to form the sink opening. For a sink frame cutout, simply drill a pilot hole and cut along the original outline.

To make the splashback, measure the lengths of the worktop edges that will rest against a wall; where two such edges meet at right angles, subtract 19 mm from one of the measurements. With a jigsaw or circular saw cut strips of core 100 mm wide to your measurements.

At this point apply tiling or a surface laminate to the core, battens and splashback using the methods shown on pages 22–27 and 30–32.

8 **Drilling and caulking for the splashback.** Support the worktop on the sawhorses and, using a 4 mm bit, drill a series of holes starting 25 mm in from the end of the worktop. Locate the holes 10 mm from the back edge of the worktop and space them 200 mm apart. Run a bead of silicone sealant round the worktop along the line formed by the holes *(above)*.

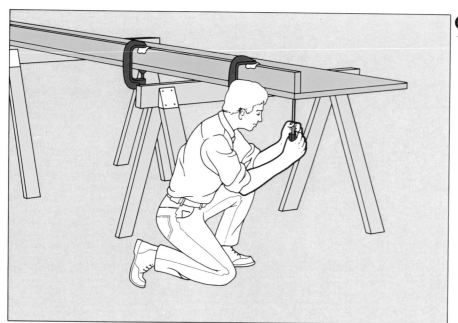

9 **Installing the splashback.** Secure the splashback in position flush with the worktop rear edge with a pair of G-cramps and hammer a 63 mm No. 10 screw into the first pre-drilled hole and into the splashback moulding. Use a screwdriver to finish driving the screw home. Repeat the procedure at every hole, repositioning the G-cramps as necessary and keeping the splashback flush with the back of the worktop. If working from below is awkward, turn the whole worktop over and screw from above.

To join strips at right angles, drive 32 mm nails spaced 20 mm apart through the back of one strip into the end of the other.

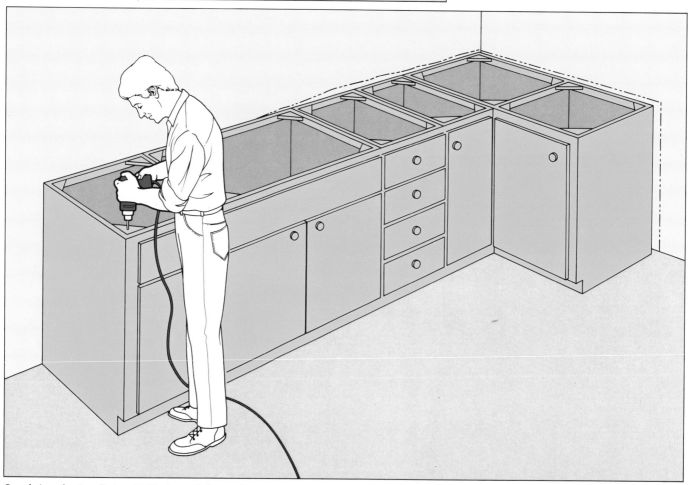

10 **Completing the installation.** Drill 4 mm holes through the centres of the braces at the outer corners of the end cabinets. Set the worktop in position and, working from below, drive No. 10 screws up through these holes into the battens above. The thickness of the braces will determine the length of the screws, but be careful not to use a screw so long that it extends through the core of the worktop and punctures the tile or laminate surface. Caution: do not use an adhesive, rather than screws, to anchor the top—prising off a glued worktop for repair or alteration is not only much more difficult than simply withdrawing the screws but is also likely to damage the cabinets and the worktop.

Fitting a Factory-Made Worktop

A mitre joint for a wide-angled corner. Cut two lengths of worktop to fit from the corner to the ends of the base units, adding 50 mm for overhang. Place both lengths on top of the units, with the longer length butted into the corner. If the corner angle is slightly wider than 90 degrees, there will be a gap between the worktops at one side. Hold a straightedge along the outer edge of the shorter length and mark the point A where the straightedge meets the edge of the longer length *(right)*. Using the straightedge, draw a line from this point A to the inside corner of the longer length B. Move both worktop lengths away from the corner.

To mark the second cutting line, butt the shorter worktop length into the corner and the longer length against it; then, following the technique described above, use a straightedge and pencil to mark a diagonal line from point C to the corner D on the shorter length *(inset)*.

Support the longer length on sawhorses and saw along the cutting line. Cut the second length in the same way. Plane both mitred ends at a slight angle to undercut the edges, then seal both edges with silicone sealant. Attach the worktop lengths to the base units with their mitred ends butted tightly against each other.

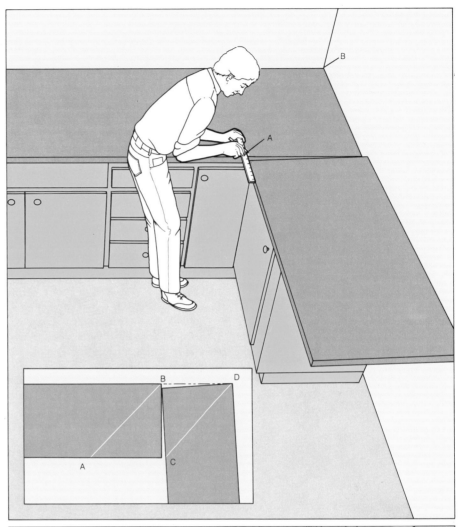

A butt joint for rounded-edge tops. Cut one length of worktop to fit along the full worktop length and the second piece to fit along the short leg only. Cut a jointing strip to the worktop depth and apply silicone sealant to both sides. Attach the jointing strip with the screws provided to the inside end of the second length of worktop *(inset)*. Install this shorter piece of worktop with the rounded edge of the jointing strip butted firmly against the front edge of the longer piece.

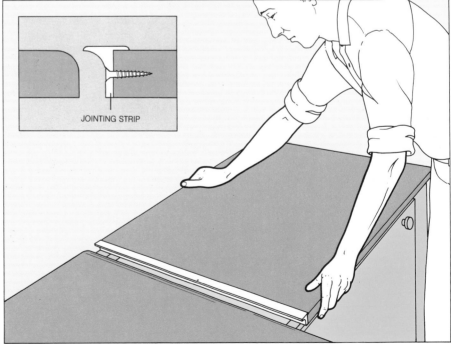

JOINTING STRIP

Fitting Cabinets to the Walls and Floors

The decor of a kitchen is set largely by the style and finish of its cabinets. Its efficiency depends mainly on their size and placement. But just as important as the cabinets themselves is the care with which they are installed. Poorly installed cabinets will sag from the start; their doors will swing open on their own or refuse to open at all. Bad installation will ruin good cabinets by wearing out their hinges and weakening their structure.

The installation job begins well before you set to work on the cabinets themselves. Unless you are fixing new cabinets to an unused wall, you must first remove the old ones. Do not simply prise them off the wall with a crowbar—old cabinets are worth saving for a workroom, darkroom or children's room. Take them down by first removing the screws that fasten the cabinets to one another, then the screws that hold the cabinets to the walls. If the slots in the screwheads are encrusted with paint, clean them with the point of a masonry nail.

With the old cabinets out of the way, mark the measurements for the new ones on the walls. Use a level to find the highest spot on the floor along these walls, and make all vertical measurements from this point. The standard height to the top of a wall cabinet is 2000 mm, or 75 or 100 mm lower if the reach is too high for you. Using the level, mark a straight line along the walls at the desired height. Next, measure the height of your cabinets and mark parallel lines along the walls for the bottoms of the wall cabinets. Finally, mark lines for the tops of the floor cabinets, adjusted if necessary to allow for a raised or lowered worktop *(page 47)*.

The width of a set of cabinets, of course, will depend upon your particular installation, but remember that ready-made cabinets will rarely fit the exact width of a wall. To fill the gaps, filler strips and tray spacers are available in the same material as the cabinets themselves. Trim the strips as necessary, and place them between cabinets of the same height—never place them at the end of a set of cabinets.

If you are attaching cabinets to a timber frame wall, you must locate the studs before drilling pilot holes for the screws. Tap along the wall with your knuckles until you hear the resonant sound that indicates the presence of a stud, then drive in a panel pin to check. Most wall studs are located 350 to 450 mm apart. Mark all the stud positions directly above and below the horizontal lines that you have marked for the tops and bottoms of the cabinets. Nonloadbearing walls that are constructed without studs are not strong enough to support heavy wall cabinets.

Walls and floors are not flat—though cabinets are made as if they were—and you will have to shim outwards or upwards to make them level. If there are conspicuous gaps between the bottom of the cabinets and the wall, hide them with a wood fillet moulding stained or painted to match the cabinets and fastened to the wall. To cover gaps between plinth and floor, use a vinyl cove moulding *(page 20)*—a wood moulding may warp from spills and cleaning.

The Right Way to Hang Cabinets

1 **Flattening a wall.** Using a straight board or spirit level, check the flatness of the walls within the lines you have marked for wall and floor cabinets. Wearing goggles, mask and hat, sand down the high spots and bulges with a sanding block and garnet paper. For very high spots use a wood chisel and a power sander, checking constantly for flatness as you work.

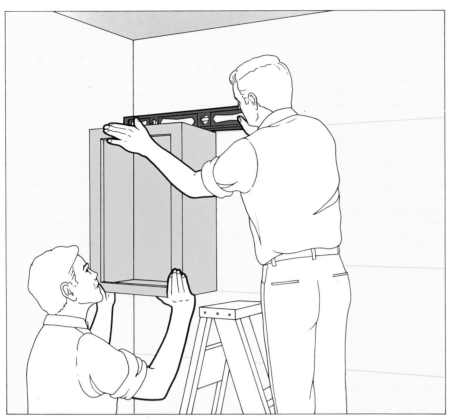

2 **Placing the first cabinet.** Remove the cabinet doors. Beginning at an inside corner, get a helper to raise the first cabinet to the horizontal line marked for the tops of the cabinets. Use a spirit level to check that the cabinet is level.

If you are working on brick or masonry walls, drill 3 mm pilot holes through the metal fittings on the back of the cabinet and just into the wall surface. Remove the cabinet, drill the wall with a tungsten carbide-tipped bit to the required depth for 50 mm screws, and insert wallplugs. Reposition the cabinet against the wall and secure it with 50 mm No. 8 or 10 screws, allowing some play for shimming *(Step 3)*. On timber frame walls, drill pilot holes through the cabinet back and directly into the studs, then fasten the cabinet to the wall with 37 mm No. 8 screws. Check the fastened cabinet for horizontal level and move the fastening screws if necessary.

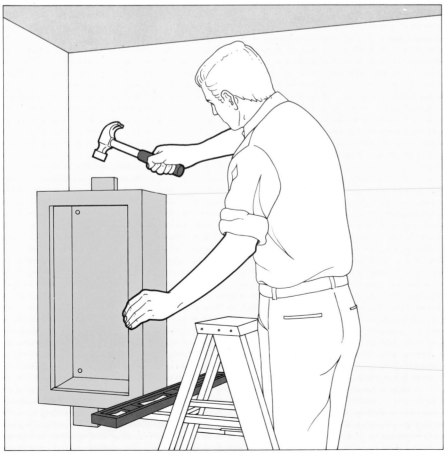

3 **Shimming for plumb.** Check the edges of the cabinet for plumb and wherever necessary drive shims between the cabinet and wall, using narrow strips of smooth wood. If the cabinet is far out of plumb, loosen screws slightly to make room for the shims. When the cabinet is plumb, tighten up the fastening screws and make a final check for both plumb and horizontal level. If you have forced the cabinet out of plumb, loosen the screws and re-shim; if the cabinet is not level, remove it and reposition the screws.

4 **Fastening cabinets together.** Install subsequent cabinets along the wall, shimming them out to the same distance from the wall as the first one. As you hang each cabinet, secure it to the preceding one with a G-cramp; protect the cabinet with pads of heavy cloth or strips of soft wood between the metal cramps and cabinets. For a cabinet up to 660 mm high, drill two 3 mm pilot holes, one-third and two-thirds of the distance from top to bottom, through the side of the front frame and into the preceding cabinet; then drive 63 mm No. 8 screws into the holes and pull the cabinets snugly together. For higher cabinets use three screws, positioned at the top, bottom and middle of the frames.

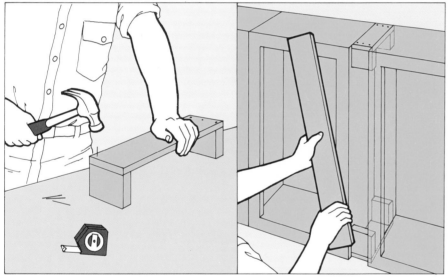

5 **Inserting a fillet.** Trim a fillet strip to bridge the gap between two installed cabinets and measure the distance from the back of the strip to the wall. Cut two pieces of 12 mm plywood to the width of the strip and the length of the distance you have measured; when fitted together at a right angle, the strip and the length of plywood should exactly match the depth of your cabinets. Cut four 25 mm blocks of wood to the width of the fillet and nail one to each end of each of the 25 mm plywood pieces with 37 or 50 mm lost-head nails to make two long, U-shaped assemblies (far left).

Fasten the plywood-and-block assemblies between the cabinets, top and bottom, with screws driven through the insides of the cabinets into the blocks. Nail the fillet to the front wood blocks with 37 or 50 mm lost-head nails, countersink the nails and cover the nail heads with filler.

Installing Floor Cabinets

Levelling with shims. Floor cabinets must be shimmed at both the wall and the floor to make them level and plumb. Slide the first cabinet into place at an inside corner, shimming it at the floor until it is level and meets the height of the line on the wall. Drive these shims in with a block of scrap wood to avoid dents and scratches in the floor or cabinet. Screw the cabinet to the wall (page 45, Step 2), making sure that pulling the cabinet towards the wall does not tilt the top. Shim along the wall to make the cabinet plumb, then tighten the screws, checking again for level and plumb. Install additional cabinets and filler strips as shown in Steps 4 and 5, above.

Setting Worktops for Your Height

The standard worktop, which rises 900 mm from the floor, can make an awkward working surface for someone considerably taller or shorter than average. Raising or lowering the top is a simple task—but remember to adjust any cutouts for pipes in the backs of cabinets to the new height.

Of the two jobs, raising a worktop is somewhat more common. Before you begin, make a sort of dry run; set strips of wood and a scrap sheet of plywood on the existing worktop, building it up to a comfortable working height. Then raise the real top to this height by either of two methods. The simpler method (*right, below*) is to remove the worktop and insert a strip of wood beneath it; the overhang of the top will hide the added strip somewhat, but the wood should match the cabinet and should be pre-stained. By another method (*right*), which calls for raising the plinth area, you can make a larger and less noticeable addition, but you will need to remove and replace the cabinet.

Worktops can be lowered by no more than half the height of the plinth, to leave adequate clearance off the ground. For the dry run, use wood strips and plywood to raise a surface lower than the worktop—a tabletop will do—to the height you want, then measure the difference between this height and the top surface of the worktop. To lower the worktop, remove the cabinet from the wall and mark off the width of the strip that must be taken from the bottom of the plinth. Draw straight lines completely around the plinth with a combination square to connect the marks, and cut along the lines with a jigsaw or circular saw. Replace the lowered cabinet with a fresh set of shims (*opposite page, below*).

Raising the plinth. Remove the cabinet from the wall and take off any moulding that may cover the plinth. Cut two strips of wood to raise the cabinet to the height you want, and to fit precisely across the front and back of the cabinet; cut two additional strips of the same thickness for the sides to fit snugly between the front and back strips. Fasten the wood strips to the bottom of the plinth with wood screws driven through the strips and into the plinth. Replace the cabinet with new shims (*opposite page, below*). To re-cover the plinth, apply a wide strip of vinyl cove moulding, following the instructions on page 20, and cut to fit if necessary.

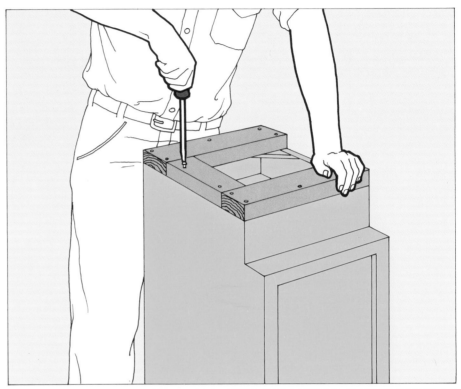

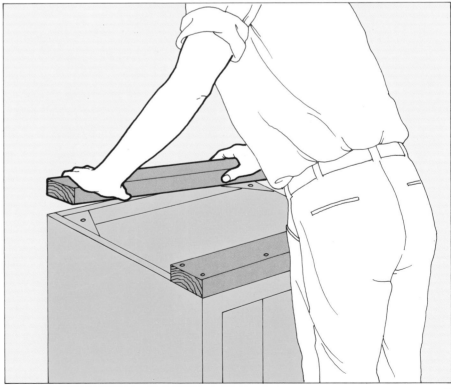

Raising the worktop. Remove the cabinet doors and unscrew the worktop from the diagonal braces in the top of the cabinet frame. Cut strips of wood to fit the top of the cabinet and screw them into place. Stain the face of the front wood strips to match the cabinet and replace the worktop with new screws long enough to bridge the new gap above the braces.

Reorganizing a Cabinet

Making full use of kitchen and bathroom cabinet space without sacrificing convenience is a challenge. Items get lost in high, inaccessible places, and extracting a saucepan or bar of soap from a low, deep cabinet requires a lot of bending. However, specialized hardware and space-saving devices can be simply and economically installed in existing cabinets to give the convenience of custom-made built-ins.

The first step in custom-fitting a cabinet to your needs is clearing the space in which to work. Shelves supported by narrow strips of wood can usually be removed by banging them with a hammer from below; the supports must then be unscrewed from the cabinet walls. If the shelves are fixed in housings in the cabinet walls, you will have to saw out a segment of each shelf and then ease out the separate pieces *(right)*. Once the permanently mounted shelving is removed, special fittings can be installed.

A variety of space-saving accessories, including drawers and a sliding rack for hanging saucepans, can be fashioned with the aid of ready-made glides *(opposite page, above)*. Refuse bins can be slotted into a drawer-frame with glides attached *(page 50)*. For storage of large trays, vertical dividers can be cut to size and slid into fixed runners.

Plastic-coated wire baskets and trays are available in many different designs, including swivelling carousel trays that make objects stored at the back of corner cabinets much more easily accessible *(page 51)*. Screws, runners and hinges for the installation of these fittings are usually supplied by the manufacturer.

Removing Old Shelves

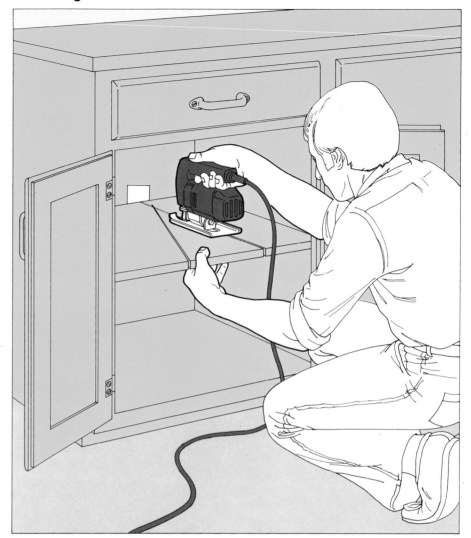

1 The first cut. Shelves are easy to remove if you saw a V that converges at the rear, making short, relief cuts—partially backing the saw in and out of the groove every few centimetres—to reduce binding of the tool as the shelf pieces sag. Use a keyhole saw to finish the rear cuts. A thin piece of plastic laminate or plywood slipped between the shelf and rear wall will protect the finish from the blade.

2 Taking out the pieces. Tap the top and bottom of the shelf halves with a hammer several times to break the glue bond that holds the shelf in the housing. Then gently work the shelf up and down until it eases out of the housing. A wet sponge placed along the housing may help to loosen the glue bond. Once both shelf parts have been removed, fill the housing with wood filler (shrinkage during drying may necessitate a second application of wood filler).

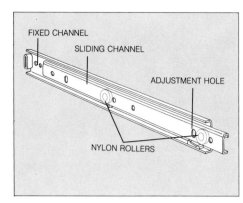

FIXED CHANNEL
SLIDING CHANNEL
ADJUSTMENT HOLE
NYLON ROLLERS

Glide-Out Conveniences

A versatile piece of hardware. Glides, which have two main components—a fixed channel that is screwed to a cabinet wall and a sliding channel that supports a drawer—can be used to mount a movable shelf, drawer or other slide-out convenience. Nested between the two channels are ball bearings and nylon rollers. Elongated screw holes allow for adjustment of the channel positions before mounting screws are tightened.

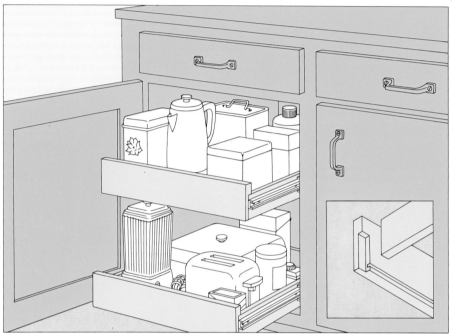

Utility drawers. Drawer frames must have sides at least 45 mm high for mounting the gliding hardware. Use a stopped rebate joint *(inset)* to withstand the stress of repeated pulling and pushing. Bottoms for most drawers can be made from thin plywood or hardboard, but if the bottoms must support heavy loads, they should be made of 12 mm plywood or tempered hardboard and should be fitted into grooves routed in the sides, back and front of the drawer.

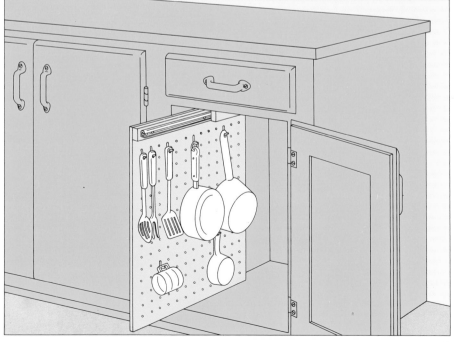

Pull-out pan rack. Mount a 50 by 25 mm strip of wood on edge to span the top of the cabinet front to back. Attach the fixed channel from a set of glides to the side of this strip, and similarly mount the sliding channel on another 50 by 25 mm strip. When the channels are engaged, the second board will slide in and out of the cabinet. Pot hooks can be screwed into the bottom of the slider, or a perforated panel can be fastened to its side as shown on the right.

A Concealed Container for Kitchen Refuse

A sliding frame. Build a strong drawer as described on page 49. Mount it upside down on glides near the top of a cabinet. Near the middle of what would ordinarily be the bottom, use a jig-saw or a keyhole saw to cut out a hole shaped and sized to support a lipped waste container at the desired level. Finally, attach a small handle to the front of the drawer.

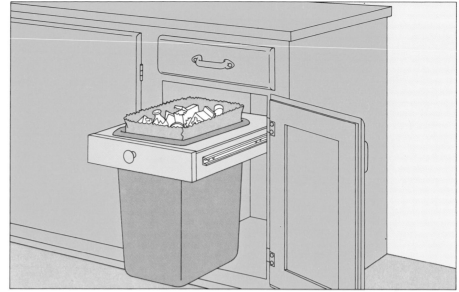

Partitions for Hard-to-Store Kitchen Utensils

Adding vertical dividers. Screw on to the bottom of the cabinet metal, plastic or wood runners—any strip with a U cross-section will serve—as long as the cabinet is deep. If the door opening extends to the underside of the cabinet top (*right*) cut 9 mm plywood as wide as the cabinet is deep and 6 mm shorter than the door opening. Slide the panels with top runners into the bottom runners; use a level to check they are vertical. Draw lines to position the upper runners. Screw the top runners along these lines.

If the door opening has a frame (*right, below*) the top runners should be suspended so the dividers can slide out. Hang the top runners between the bottom edge of the fascia in front and a crosswise level board screwed to the rear wall.

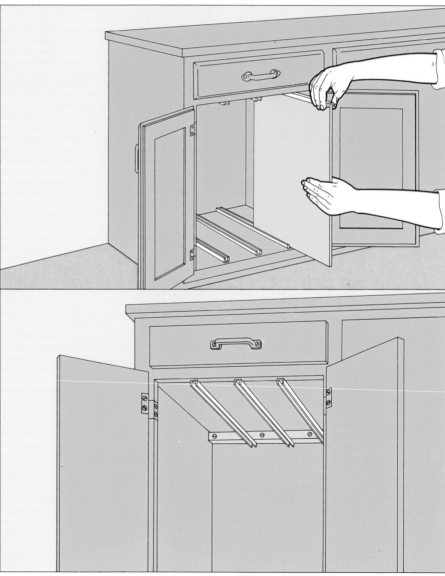

Wire Baskets for Easy Access

Sliding baskets on fixed runners. Mark the positions for fixing the side runners to the inside of the cabinet; use a spirit level to check that they are aligned horizontally. Secure the runners with the screws provided. Plastic-coated wire baskets are available in several widths and depths to match standard cabinet dimensions. For storing vegetables, the baskets can be held in freestanding frames mounted on castors.

A wire basket fixed to a door. Before securing the basket, remove the cabinet door. Reattach it with strong hinges that will support extra weight. If necessary, cut back the existing shelf or shelves inside the cabinet with a jigsaw to allow room for the basket when the door is closed. Attach the basket to the back of the door with small screws or hooks; make sure they are not longer than the thickness of the cabinet door.

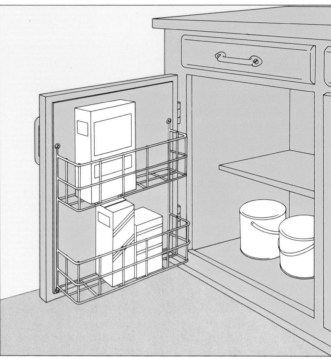

A swivelling tray for a corner unit. Measure the height of the tallest objects to be stored in the upper carousel tray. Hold one hinge bracket against the cabinet carcass, slightly farther from the top than the measurement you have taken, and mark the positions of the screw holes. Fix the hinge bracket to the carcass with the screws provided. Attach the carousel tray by slotting the hinge pin through the holes in the bracket and the back of the tray *(top inset)*.

Secure the lower carousel tray in the same way, or alternatively attach it to the cabinet door so that it is pulled forward automatically when the door is opened. Slot a shelf follower under one of the straight bars and secure the follower to the door with screws *(bottom inset)*.

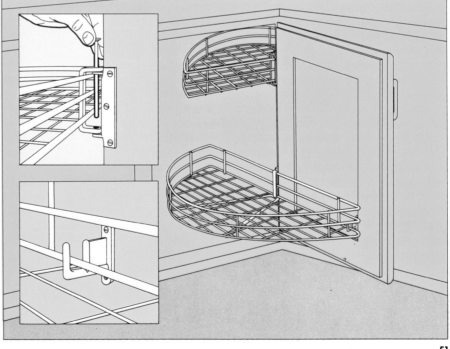

Clearing the Air of Odours, Smoke and Moisture

The insulated walls, close-fitting doors and double-glazed windows of a typical, well-constructed house are usually effective in preserving heat, but they can cause problems by restricting the free movement of air. The consequences of poor ventilation are particularly apparent in kitchens and bathrooms, where cooking odours and greasy smoke can pollute the air and water vapour can condense into moisture that mists mirrors and windows and, more importantly, damages walls and floors.

In bathrooms, an axial fan mounted in a wall can extract air from large areas and help to eliminate condensation (opposite page). To encourage a continuous circulation of air, install the fan on the opposite side of the room to the main door. The fan should be positioned close to the bath and as high as possible, to take advantage of the rising currents of hot air into which steam and odours are drawn. Some fans are designed to be installed in a window, which eliminates the chore of knocking a hole through a wall, but a wall-mounted fan reduces condensation more effectively by drawing moist air away from the cold glass surface of windows.

The area and number of air changes per hour recommended for a particular room determine the amount of ventilation required, and you may wish to seek professional advice before purchasing a fan. On some models, the type and size of room for which the fan is suitable is indicated on the packaging. The simplest axial fans serve to extract air only and have one speed; more sophisticated fans have two or three speeds and have reversible motors that can draw in fresh air when required. Most fans are fitted with back-draught shutters to stop unpleasant draughts being blown back into the room when the fan is switched off. In a bathroom or W.C. without windows you should install a fan that is controlled by the door or light switch and that continues to function for a set period after you have used the room.

Axial fans must be connected to the household electricity supply through a double-pole fused isolating switch. Follow the manufacturer's instructions carefully when wiring the cable to the fan terminals; if you have little experience of electrical work, call in a professional.

The most appropriate form of ventilation for kitchens is a cooker hood fitted with a centrifugal fan that sucks in air from a well-defined, localized area. Depending on how it is installed, a cooker hood can either recirculate the air in a kitchen or extract it through a duct in an outside wall. For recirculation, the hood sucks in air over the cooker and draws it through two filters—a metal or plastic filter for removing grease and a carbon filter for removing odours—before returning the cleaned air to the kitchen through an outlet in the top of the cooker hood. Extraction works more effectively because the cooker hood removes not only grease and odours but steam as well, and so protects the surfaces of walls and ceilings from condensation.

No structural alteration is necessary when installing a hood for recirculation; installation for extraction (page 54), on the other hand, involves making a hole in an outside wall and securing ducting. Ideally, the duct should lead directly from the cooker hood through the outside wall (page 55, above); if the cooker is placed against an inner wall or in the centre of the kitchen, however, you will have to install a series of ducts to channel the extracted air to the nearest outside wall (page 55, below). Plan to install the ducts so that you create the least possible resistance to the air flow: use rigid heat-resistant plastic ducts for long runs, and keep the route as straight as the kitchen layout permits—each right-angle turn causes as much resistance as a metre of straight ducting. Where possible, slope horizontal ducts 10 degrees downwards (a drop of 50 mm per metre length) to prevent moisture from condensation inside the duct flowing back into the hood. Rigid plastic ducts are available in lengths of one metre, and can be cut to size with a hacksaw; connectors, elbow joints, wall plates and transition fittings for joining round to rectangular ducts are sold individually or in kits. For short runs and for ducting through enclosed areas such as kitchen cabinets, flexible plastic ducts are easier to manipulate. If over four metres of ducting is required, install a cooker hood with a higher pressure development capacity than standard models.

Cooker hoods are available in several designs. The cooker hood shown on page 54 is the basic conventional model; it can be fixed either directly to the wall or to the underside of a wall-mounted kitchen cabinet. Hob lights and fire shields that provide protection against accidental cooking fat fires are standard fittings. Most models are supplied with a length of cable already attached, and must be connected to the mains electricity supply via a plug and socket or a double-pole fused isolating switch. Whichever design of cooker hood or method of installation you choose, the base of the hood must be situated at least 600 mm above an electric hob, or 700 mm above a gas hob, to ensure the hood functions safely and with maximum efficiency.

Before carrying out any maintenance on a cooker hood, switch off or disconnect the electrical supply. The grease filter of a cooker hood should be removed every 10 to 15 days, and cleaned in hot, soapy water. If the hood is installed for recirculation, the carbon filter will normally need to be replaced after 12 to 18 months.

Both fans and cooker hoods are usually supplied with all the screws, bolts and mounting brackets necessary for correct installation, together with comprehensive fitting instructions. The most demanding stage in the installation process is usually knocking a hole through an outside wall (opposite page, above). Check that there are no electricity cables or gas or water pipes sunk into the wall where you plan to locate the duct—it is wise to switch off the power supply to the room you are working in before drilling the initial hole—and always wear safety goggles when drilling or chiselling to protect your eyes from any flying particles.

Installing a Fan in a Wall

1 Cutting through the wall. Hold one end of the fan sleeve against the wall and draw round its circumference with a pencil. At the centre of the circular outline, use a long masonry bit to drill a hole right through the wall. With a standard length masonry bit, drill several holes round the inside of the circular outline *(right)*, then use a hammer and cold chisel to chip out the masonry or brickwork inside the hole to about half the thickness of the wall. On the outside of the wall, use the exit hole made by the long masonry bit as a guide for drawing a matching circular outline. Drill holes round the outline, then chisel out the brick or masonry until the hole is clear.

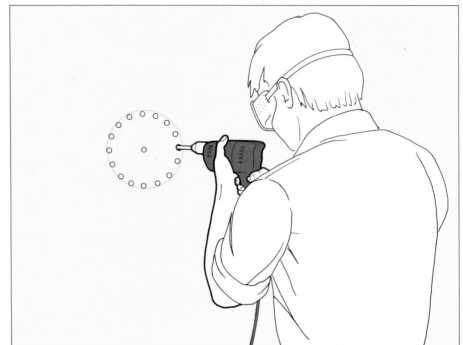

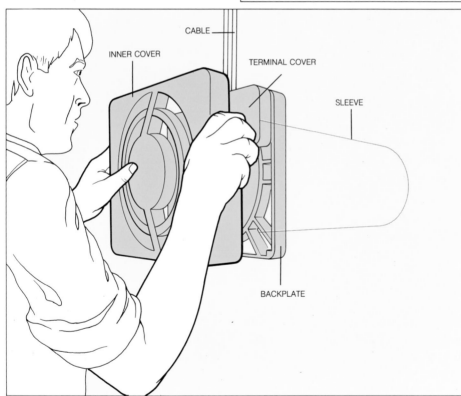

CABLE

INNER COVER

TERMINAL COVER

SLEEVE

BACKPLATE

2 Mounting the fan. Insert the fan sleeve into the hole in the wall. If the sleeve is longer than the thickness of the wall, cut off the excess material with a hacksaw. Secure the sleeve by pointing round both ends with mortar. Slot the backplate into the inside end of the sleeve and mark the positions of the screw holes on the wall; remove the backplate, drill holes and insert plugs, then secure the backplate with the screws provided. With a hammer and cold chisel, chip out a channel for the connecting cable. Following the manufacturer's instructions, connect the cable to the terminals in the backplate; if in doubt, consult a professional electrician. Clip the inner cover containing the fan motor to the backplate *(above)*.

3 Completing the assembly. Cover the cable with a metal or plastic conduit, then make good the channel in the wall by filling it with plaster. On the outside of the wall, slot the back-draught shutter into the end of the sleeve, mark the positions of the screw holes, drill and plug holes in the wall and then secure the shutter with the screws provided *(above)*.

Mounting a Cooker Hood for Extraction

1 Marking the extraction and fixing the holes. Strip off the blanking plate masking the outlet hole at the rear of the cooker hood. Make a cardboard template to mark the positions of the screw holes and rear outlet hole on the wall *(right)*. Check with a spirit level that the screw holes are aligned horizontally.

If the hood is to be fixed to the underside of a cabinet, mark the positions of the four screw holes on the cabinet bottom; in the same way, mark the outline of the top outlet hole on the cabinet bottom if the cooker hood is to be installed for top extraction.

TEMPLATE

TOP EXTRACTION

REAR EXTRACTION

2 Fitting the duct spigot. At the positions you have marked, drill holes in the wall for the mounting screws. For extraction through an outside wall, cut a hole in the wall at the marked position *(page 53, Step 1)* and install a duct as described opposite, above. Slot a duct spigot into the rear outlet hole in the cooker hood *(right)*.

For fixing the hood to a cabinet and for top extraction, drill holes in the cabinet bottom for the bolts provided and cut out a hole with a jigsaw for the duct spigot.

DUCT SPIGOT

3 Securing the hood. Insert plugs and screws in the holes drilled in the wall and tighten the screws until their heads are 5 mm from the wall. Lift the cooker hood on to the screws so that their heads engage firmly with the keyhole slots in the rear of the hood *(right)*. If the hood tilts forward, remove the front access panel and thread two bolts through the holes in the bottom of the rear panel until the hood hangs correctly *(inset)*. For fixing to a cabinet, secure the hood to the cabinet bottom with the nuts and bolts provided.

If a socket outlet is conveniently located, fit a 13 amp plug protected by a 3 amp fuse to the end of the cable; alternatively, fit a double-pole fused isolating switch. Follow the manufacturer's instructions carefully when making the wiring connections. If in doubt, consult an electrician.

Two Routes for Ducting

Direct ducting through a wall. If the cooker hood is mounted on an outside wall, mark the outline of the rear outlet hole directly on to the wall *(opposite page, Step 1)*. Following the instructions on page 53, Step 1, make a hole through the wall to take ducting of the diameter specified by the cooker hood manufacturer. Cut a length of rigid duct to the thickness of the wall and secure it in the wall by pointing with mortar at both ends. When the cooker hood is mounted, its duct spigot will slot neatly into the prepared duct in the wall. Mount a protective wall grille over the outside end of the duct.

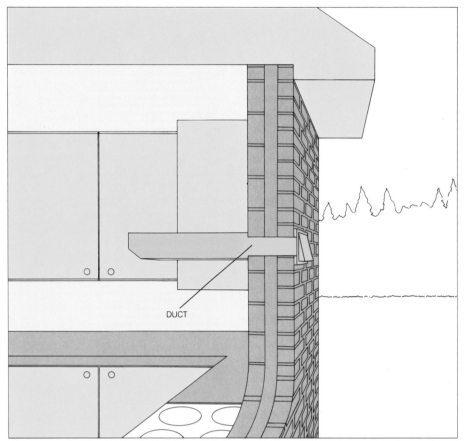

DUCT

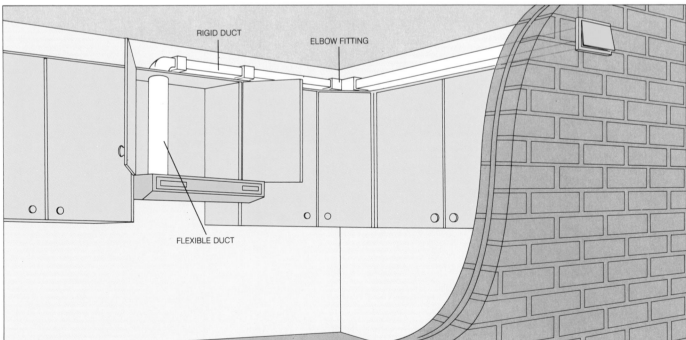

RIGID DUCT   ELBOW FITTING

FLEXIBLE DUCT

An extended run. Fumes extracted by a cooker hood mounted on an inside wall must be led to the nearest outside wall through a series of connecting ducts. If the hood is mounted beneath a cabinet *(above)* cut a length of flexible duct to lead from the bottom to the top of the cabinet, and slot it into the cooker hood duct spigot. Mark and cut a hole in the top of the cabinet to join the flexible duct to a transition fitting on top of the cabinet. Slot together sections of rigid ducting with connectors and elbow joints where necessary until the nearest outside wall is reached.

Mark and cut a hole in the wall, as described on page 53, Step 1, to lead the ducting outside, and mount either a single-flap louvre and cover or a wall grille over the end of the duct.

Exposed ducting along the top of kitchen cabinets can be boxed in.

Making a Serving Hatch for Easier Access

When an adjoining kitchen and dining room have no communicating door, an easy way of creating direct access between them is to cut a serving hatch through the wall. Making the hole for a hatchway is quite straightforward, whether the wall is constructed of timber studs and plasterboard, brick or block. Determine the type of wall by rapping it with your fist: a stud wall sounds loud and hollow, a brick or block wall gives a dull, solid sound.

Before starting any work, mark the position of the opening on the wall, allowing extra space for the frame. A serving hatch should be at least one metre above the floor and should have an opening large enough to pass a tray through, a good size is 700 mm wide by 500 mm high.

The size and position of the hatch may be limited by the location of plugs, switches and wiring: wiring usually travels vertically from switches and sockets. Always turn off the power to the relevant circuit when working on a wall containing wiring.

In a stud partition wall, the location of the hatch will depend to some extent on the position of the studs. Modern walls are normally constructed of 100 by 50 mm studs set 400 or 450 mm apart from centre to centre, giving a space of 350 or 400 mm between studs; studs in older houses tend to be spaced closer together.

On a masonry wall *(pages 58–59)* it is best to decide the exact location of the hatch once the plaster has been removed, and the bricks or blocks exposed. Then the outline can be adjusted to coincide wherever possible with mortar joints which will allow the removal of whole bricks or blocks rather than pieces.

A brick or block wall must have a lintel to support the masonry above the opening. The type of lintel you use must depend on whether or not the wall is load-bearing *(page 92)*. For a non-loadbearing wall, a lintel which consists of two 100 by 50 mm lengths of timber placed side by side will be strong enough; if the wall is load-bearing,

a 110 by 50 mm pre-stressed concrete lintel must be installed. The lintel must extend at least 100 mm beyond each side of the hatchway opening.

Bricks or blocks can be knocked out with a lump hammer and bolster, but for the lintel, where careful removal of masonry is important, use a jointing chisel. Alternatively, masonry can be cut through with a saw: for lightweight blocks use an old rip saw. A masonry power saw will cut any brick or block. Cutting through blocks or bricks gives a neat result, but creates a lot of dust—wear goggles and a dust mask.

Once the hole has been made, the frame for the hatchway is constructed in the same way whether for a stud or masonry wall *(pages 60–61)*: four 32 mm thick pieces of wood cut to the thickness of the finished wall are joined together using rebate and housing joints, and a small shelf is fitted to the bottom to allow trays to rest in the opening. The hatchway is finished off with architrave and, if desired, a pair of doors.

Cutting Holes in Stud Walls

1 Locating the wall studs. Most wall studs are spaced 400 or 450 mm apart, centre to centre, although the spacing may be less in older houses. Once you find one, quick measurements on the surface of the wall will locate the rest. It is sometimes possible to find a stud simply by tapping the wall, but a surer method is to drill a small, inconspicuous hole at an acute angle along the wall's surface. Feed a piece of stiff wire at least 500 mm long into the hole *(right)* until it meets resistance—a stud. Grasp the wire where it enters the wall and withdraw it from the hole. Hold the wire just outside the hole and at the same angle to the wall at which it entered. The edge of the stud lies behind the point where the tip of the wire meets the wall.

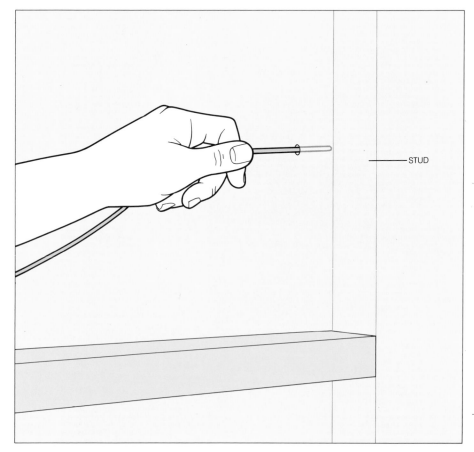

STUD

2 **Removing intervening studs.** Locate the two studs on either side of the proposed opening. Between them mark on the wall horizontal lines 50 mm above and 50 mm below the proposed location of the hatch. With a trimming knife cut out the wall surface bounded by these lines and the two side studs. At the four corners of the opening drill holes through to the other side of the wall. Working in the other room, pencil the outline of the opening by joining up the holes; cut out the wall surface and knock out any noggings—horizontal timbers between the studs—with a hammer. With a handsaw, sever the intervening studs flush with the top and the bottom of the opening.

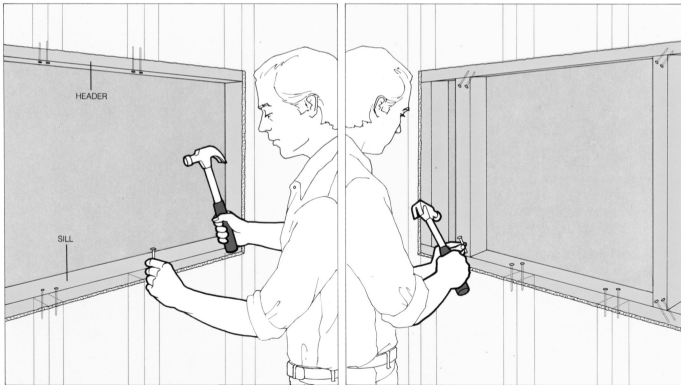

HEADER

SILL

3 **Lining the opening.** Install a header and a sill of 100 by 50 mm timber segments nailed to the severed ends of the intervening studs; use a pair of 100 mm round-wire nails for each stud *(above)*. For additional strength, toenail the header and sill to the side studs.

4 **Narrowing the opening.** If the hatch is to be narrower than the opening thus created, first nail 100 by 50 mm vertical pieces to the studs. Then cut two 100 by 50 mm pieces the height of the opening and toenail them to the sill and header on each side of the desired hatch *(above)*. Fill the spaces around the opening with plasterboard patches nailed to the vertical 100 by 50 mm pieces. Skim over with finishing plaster *(page 9)*.

Knocking a Hole in Brick

1 Inserting the needles. Using a spirit level as a straightedge, pencil the proposed position of the hatch and lintel on the wall, then remove the plaster within this area with a lump hammer and bolster. Adjust the dimensions so that the outline coincides with horizontal and vertical mortar joints; remove a little more plaster if necessary. With the lump hammer and bolster, make two holes about 80 mm square through the wall about 300 mm above the outline and 300 mm in. Push a 75 by 75 mm timber needle, approximately 1 metre long, through each hole until they protrude by equal amounts on either side of the wall.

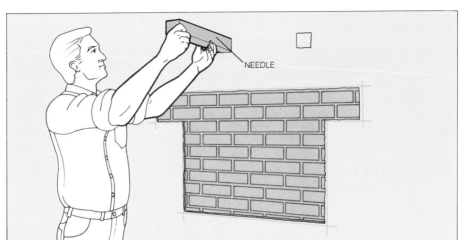

2 Bracing the needles. Measure the distance from the top of one of the holes to the floor, deduct 75 mm (the thickness of the needle) and cut four 100 by 50 mm props to this length. Support the needles on both sides of the wall by jamming a prop under each end. If the floor is of wood, place a sole plate between the props and the floor. If the props are loose, use wedges to tighten them; hammer the wedges together until the props are just tight and pushing the needles up so that they take the weight of the bricks above; be careful not to overtighten them. Toenail the needles to the props *(right)*; pin the wedges to the sole plate *(inset)*.

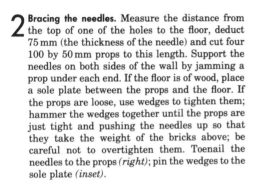

3 Knocking out a rectangle for the lintel. Holding the bolster at a slight angle to the wall, chip out the mortar lines and remove enough bricks or blocks to accommodate the lintel. Start at the top of the outline and work downwards, removing one course at a time.

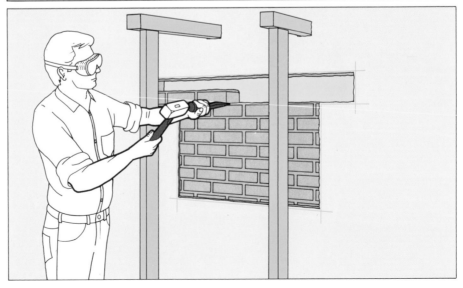

4 **Installing the lintel.** Mix four parts of soft sand with one of cement, add water and stir to a stiff consistency. Use a trowel to spread the mortar 20 mm thick along the bottom of the opening, either side of the hatchway outline. With a helper, lift and carefully place the lintel on the prepared mortar bed, tapping it down until it is level. Check it with a spirit level.

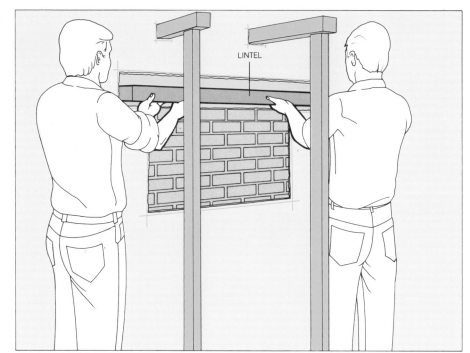

5 **Building the lintel in.** Cut bricks or blocks to fit the gaps round the lintel, allowing for mortar joints, and build them into the wall. Pack the mortar well into the joints. Place a straightedge on the intact plaster and slide it across the newly built-up area to check that the plaster stands proud of the brickwork by at least 15 mm. Push any protruding bricks back in place.

Leave the props and needles in position for three days until the mortar hardens. After removing them, brick up the holes.

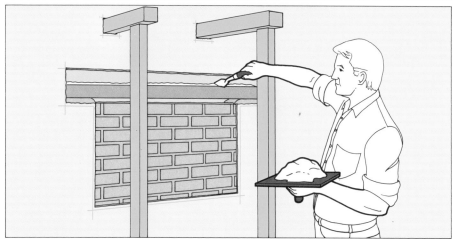

6 **Knocking out the hatchway.** Use the lump hammer and bolster to chisel down the vertical lines of the hatchway, working first from one side of the wall and then the other. Start at the top of the hatchway and knock out whole bricks or blocks to make the opening. Trim any protruding bricks by placing the bolster on the brick and giving it a sharp blow with the hammer (right).

Plaster over the bricked-up needle holes and the lintel to the edge of the opening.

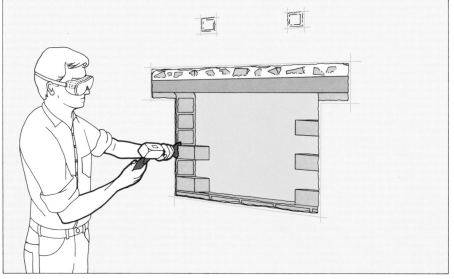

Building the Hatchway

1 Cutting the frame. For the top and bottom of the frame, cut two pieces of 32 mm thick wood the width of the wall and the length of the hatch plus 50 mm. With a mortise gauge, score a 6 by 6 mm housing across the width of each piece, 51 mm from either end. Saw to the bottom of the gauge lines and chisel out the housing. Then, using a router, cut a 10 by 10 mm housing along the centre of the outside edge of the bottom piece. For the sides cut two 32 mm thick pieces, 12 mm longer than the inside height of the hatch. With a mortise gauge, score a 26 by 6 mm rebate across each end. Cut out the rebate, first sawing down the grain, and then across it. For the shelf, cut a 110 by 32 mm piece the length of the bottom of the hatch. Then score and cut a rebate 10 by 11 mm along each side of one edge, to leave a tongue 10 by 10 mm in the middle.

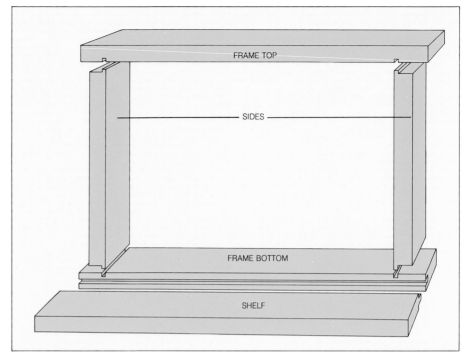

FRAME TOP

SIDES

FRAME BOTTOM

SHELF

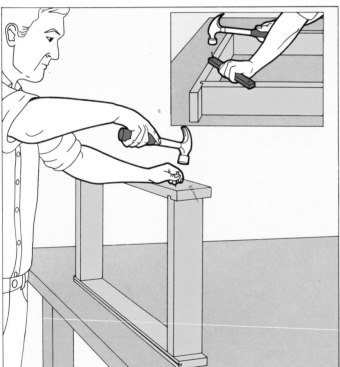

2 Assembling the frame. Join the housings and rebates of the frame with PVA glue and dovetail two 75 mm round-wire nails into each joint *(above)*. Check that the frame is square by measuring the diagonals: they should be equal. To keep the frame square until the glue sets, tack a brace across one corner *(inset)*. When the glue has set, saw off the horns on the two sides of the frame and remove the brace.

WOOD STRIPS

3 Mounting the frame. Set the frame into the wall opening. To ensure a snug fit, pack wood strips between the frame and the wall; this is not necessary for a stud wall. Check with a spirit level that the frame is level.

If the wall is brick, secure each side of the frame by dovetailing two pairs of 63 mm No. 10 steel countersunk screws about 125 mm from the corners *(above)*. For a block or timber wall, dovetail two pairs of 75 mm cut nails.

4 **Hanging the doors.** Glue the shelf to the base of the frame. Cut two doors from 18 mm blockboard and lip them with 12 mm hardwood. Attach a pair of 75 mm steel or brass butt hinges to each door and screw the hinges to the frame *(right)*. From the other side of the hatch nail a doorstop of three 37 by 10 mm battens around the top and sides of the frame next to the closed doors *(far right)*. Ask a helper to hold the hatch doors shut as you fix the stop.

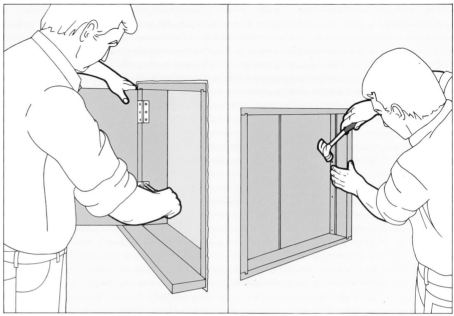

5 **Attaching the architrave.** Using 37 mm oval or lost-head nails, pin a 37 by 12 mm wood architrave around the top and sides, about 6 mm from the edge of the frame, to hide the joint between the frame and the wall. Repeat on the side of the hatch that has no shelf. Pin architrave along the bottom edge on this side.

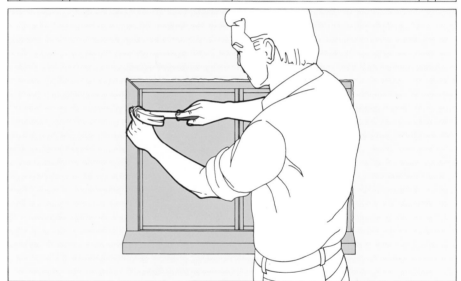

6 **Finishing the hatch.** Screw magnetic catches to the top inside corners of the doors and to their corresponding positions on the inside edge of the doorstop. Screw door handles to both sides of the doors *(right)*. Sand down and paint with primer. undercoat and gloss.

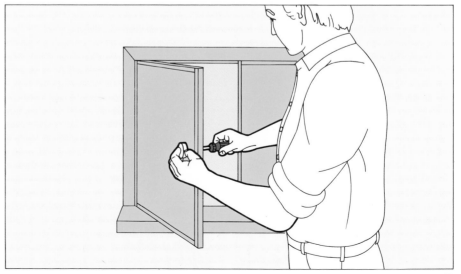

Making a Sauna from a Box, a Bench and a Heater

A sauna, an insulated wood box that provides a steam bath, can be tucked into a corner of a bathroom, basement or garage—or expanded to fill most of a spare bedroom. The top is always low—1800 to 2000 mm is ideal—so a sauna can fit under any normal ceiling. The floor space for a one to two-person unit need only be just over one square metre. A family-sized unit in Finland, where saunas were invented, covers approximately 3·5 square metres and will hold a two-tiered bench with both seats large enough for lying on: 500 mm wide and 1800 mm long.

A modern unit operates with an electric heater. Because the panelling is unfinished wood, it remains comfortable to touch even when the heater brings the bath to the ideal 88°C.

Building the sauna calls only for simple woodworking and wiring. The walls can be framed and the ceiling fabricated on the floor, then raised into place *(right)*. The bench frame, however, must be assembled in place *(page 65)* because it is permanently anchored to the wall opposite or beside the heater. The bench seat is made separately and is removable for cleaning. The tongue and groove panelling and the bench should be made of resin-free softwood, preferably spruce, and must be 12 to 14 per cent kiln-dried timber; resin ducts and sappy knots in unseasoned timber get hot and exude sticky liquid. To avoid the danger of burns, all the nail heads must be punched and the screws must be countersunk.

Room walls can provide outer covering for one or two sauna walls, but the others are sheathed with plywood, oil-tempered hardboard, plasterboard or tongue and groove panelling. The floor under the box may be left bare if it is concrete, or covered with a simple wood grid or vinyl sheet.

Kiln-dried timber may be ordered from your timber merchant, but the heater and special sauna door must be obtained from a sauna dealer. Check that the heater you choose will not overload your electrical system. The manufacturer will supply instructions for connecting the heater but you should leave the consumer unit connections to a professional. The door, which can be either solid wood with a double-strength window to admit light, or all glass, comes prehung *(page 66)*. By buying the heater and door in advance, you can plan their locations and requisite framing when you plot dimensions for the sauna. At the same time you can position the inlet and outlet vents *(page 66)*. You may also require other accessories such as porcelain-based light fittings, a thermometer and an adjustable vent hatch for the air outlet.

Constructing the Box

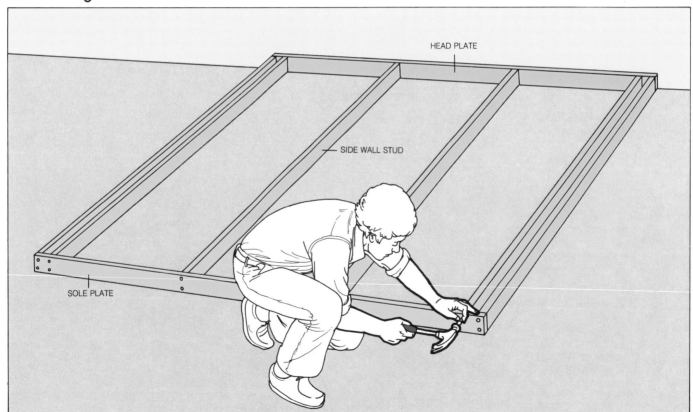

1 Framing the walls. Working on the floor, assemble each frame of 100 by 50s. The head and sole plates for the front and back wall frames are cut to the inside width of the sauna; plates for the side walls are 200 mm longer than the inside depth. Cut studs 100 mm shorter than the ceiling height, and set them between the ends of the plates and at intervals of about 400 mm. For the door, leave a space of 12 mm wider than the jamb. Secure the head and sole plates to the studs with 100 mm round-wire nails. For each side frame, add an extra stud 50 mm inside each end stud. For the door header, nail a 100 by 50 crosswise between the studs 10 mm above the finished height of the top of the doorjamb.

2 **Erecting the wall frames.** After removing the skirting board *(page 10)*, set the back frame flat against the room wall, leaving a 100 mm space at the end for a side frame if you plan to locate the sauna in a corner.

Using a spirit level, plumb the back frame and add packing or shims as needed to make it absolutely vertical. Toenail the head into each stud of the room wall, or secure it with masonry nails spaced 450 mm apart if the wall is concrete.

If the floor is wood, secure the sole plate with 75 mm nails 400 mm apart. If the floor is concrete, use a 6 mm masonry bit to drill through the plate into the floor at 400 mm intervals, tap in plastic plugs and secure the plate with 75 mm No. 10 screws. Nail the side wall frames to the back frame at the corners. Set the front frame between the sides and nail. Anchor these frames to the floor, then saw out the sole plate between the doorframe studs.

3 **Fabricating the ceiling.** The ceiling is a 100 by 50 mm frame sheathed in plywood, filled with insulation and panelled inside with tongue and groove *(below)*. Make front and back plates as long as the outside width of the sauna, joists 100 mm shorter; nail joists between plates every 600 mm. Nail 6 mm plywood to the joists at 300 mm intervals. Turn the ceiling over. Staple 75 mm mineral wool insulation or fibreglass batts between joists, vapour barrier towards you. Nail boards over the insulation, at right angles to the joists, setting the groove side of the first board flush with the frame edge. Drive four 35 mm lost-head nails along the frame edge. Then drive and countersink nails at a 45-degree angle into each of the joists through the corner at the base of the tongue *(inset)*. Nail successive boards only along the tongue side. Cut the tongue edge off the last board within 12 mm of the edge of the frame; nail the board to the frame edge.

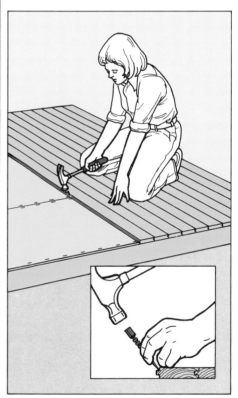

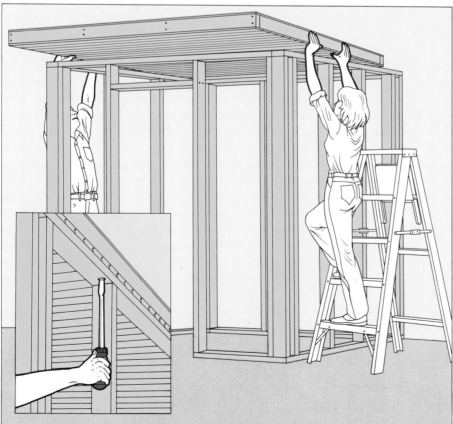

4 **Installing the ceiling.** After drilling two 6 mm holes in the head plate of each wall frame, 20 mm from the outer edge and a third of the way from each corner, set the ceiling on top of the wall frames, panelled side down. Align the edges. Then drill 2 mm pilot holes into the ceiling through the 6 mm holes in the wall frames. Insert 6 mm coach screws 75 mm long, using a screwdriver to tighten them securely *(inset)*.

Finishing the Walls

1 Bringing in power. Run high temperature cable as specified by the manufacturer from the consumer unit to the heater, which is usually placed against the wall containing the door or on a side wall as close to the door as possible; consider where you will position the vents *(Step 2, below)* before positioning the heater. If you lead the cable in from a room wall, drill a 20 mm hole through each stud of the side and front frame to the heater location. For a heater with built-in controls and relays, drill the holes 300 mm above the sole plate or at heater mounting height specified by the manufacturer. For a heater with separate controls, drill the holes at a convenient height for mounting the control and relay box outside the sauna.

If you lead the cable in from the room ceiling, drill a 20 mm hole just inside the top edge of the sauna ceiling and through the head of the wall frame next to the stud that lies nearest to the location of the heater.

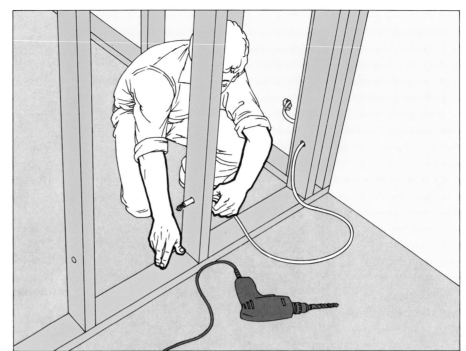

2 Venting and insulating. The sauna walls are filled with mineral wool insulation or with fibreglass batts—foil vapour barrier to the inside of the sauna—then vented and sheathed with cladding. Before filling in with insulation against an existing room wall, fix a few timber battens to ensure a 25 mm air gap between the insulation and the wall. Cut a 120 by 100 mm hole about 150 mm above the floor in the wall behind or next to the heater and snip a matching hole through the insulation. Cut another 120 by 100 mm vent hole in the wall opposite the heater and about 100 mm below the ceiling. Working on the outside of the sauna, cover each hole with a metal or plastic grille. Both vents should open into the same room, which itself must be well ventilated.

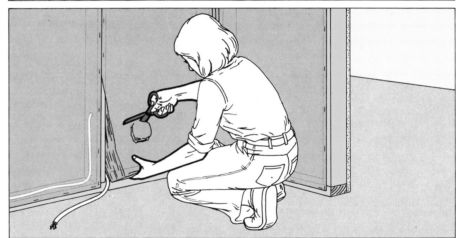

3 Panelling the walls. Measure the height of the back wall, deduct the width of one tongue of your panelling and then divide the total by the width of a panelling strip. If the last strip will be less than half a board, increase its width to half and use a circular or table saw to rip the amount of the increase from the groove side of the first strip. Panel from the bottom up. Rip the back edge of the tongue side of the top strip to a 45-degree angle *(inset)*; place the groove of the top strip over the tongue of the preceding strip and tap the board to swing it back against the studs. Nail the top strip into the head plate of the wall near the ceiling. Punch the nail heads. Panel the front wall and then the side walls similarly, cutting the strips before securing them to leave the vent holes exposed. If your heater has built-in controls, drill a 20 mm hole and feed the cable through the strip at the heater mounting location before securing the strip. Fix a grille to the inlet and an adjustable vent hatch to the outlet.

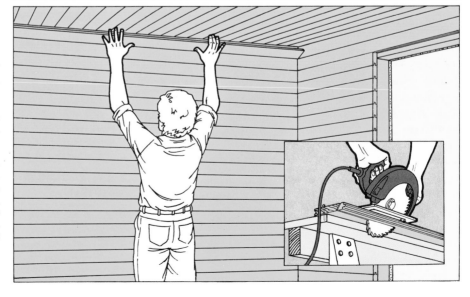

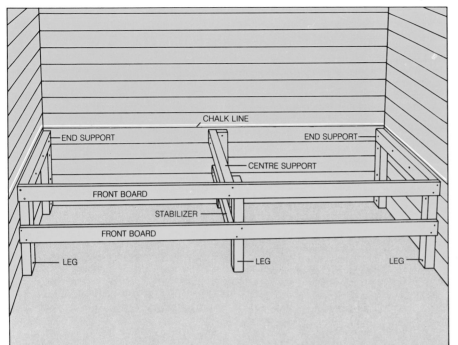

Building a Single Bench

1 **Constructing the frame.** Using 70 by 45 mm planed timber, make seat end supports 22 mm shorter than the overall bench width and legs 92 mm shorter than the overall bench height. Nail the end supports and legs to the side walls. Provide additional support at 900 mm intervals—a 70 by 45 mm support and a 70 by 22 mm stabilizer, both cut 22 mm shorter than the overall bench width, and legs 22 mm shorter than bench height. Face-nail the legs to the ends of the support, then turn the assembly over and nail the stabilizer to the legs 150 mm from the bottoms. Secure the back leg of the centre support to the back wall with lost-head nails. To tie the whole frame together, cut two 70 by 22 mm pieces the length of the bench and nail these boards to the front of the supports at the top and 150 mm above the floor.

CHALK LINE
END SUPPORT
END SUPPORT
CENTRE SUPPORT
FRONT BOARD
STABILIZER
FRONT BOARD
LEG
LEG
LEG

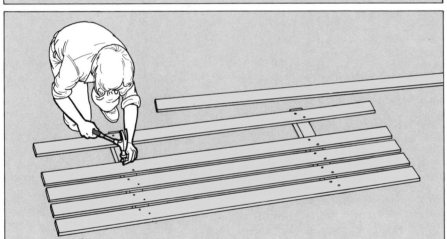

2 **Assembling the seat.** Using 70 by 45 mm pieces, cut a cleat—22 mm shorter than the overall bench width—to fit inside the seat between each pair of legs. To find how many 70 by 22 mm slats you need, divide the bench depth, in mm, by 70. Cut the slats 6 mm shorter than the length of the bench. Lay the cleats in position on the floor and arrange the slats across them. Let the front slat overlap the front of .the cleats by 22 mm and leave 12 mm of cleat protruding behind the back slat; space the remaining slats evenly between the front and back. Round the top edges of the slats with glass paper, then nail the slats to the cleats with 37 mm lost-head nails. Punch all nail heads. Place the seat on the bench frame; do not fasten it, so you can remove it for cleaning.

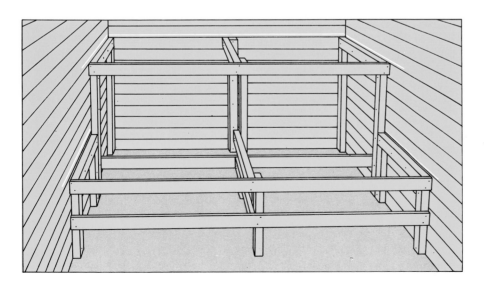

Adding a Second Tier

Connecting the tiers. Frame a simple bench *(Step 1, above)* 800 mm high, nailing the lower front board to the back of the legs rather than to the front. Then, in front of the first, assemble end supports and legs for another simple bench 400 mm high. To support the front bench at each 900 mm interval, cut a 70 by 45 mm support and a 70 by 22 mm stabilizer 70 mm longer than the seat depth. For each support, cut one leg 400 mm long and nail it to the front end of the support. Nail the back end of the support to the front leg of the support on the back bench. Nail the stabilizer to the front leg of the front support and the front leg of the back bench. Attach front boards to the front frame. Then make two identical seats for the frames *(Step 2, above)*.

Installing a Door and Heater Fence

Installing the prehung door. Position the door unit in its rough opening to open outwards, wedging it in place with pieces of cardboard. Insert two evenly spaced wood packers between the top of the jamb and the header and three along each side of the jamb to maintain a 6 mm clearance between the jamb and the outer stud frame. (On the hinge side of the jamb, the packers cannot be evenly spaced; set a packer just below each hinge and a third packer midway between them.) Drive a pair of 75 mm oval or lost-head nails through the jamb and each packer into the frame. Knock off the protruding ends of the packers and remove the cardboard strips to free the door. Nail the interior and exterior doorcasing around the jamb with 37 mm oval or lost-head nails.

Building a heater fence. A wooden fence set at least 100 mm from the heater shields it. Cut a pair of planed 45 by 22 mm fence rails to reach from the wall 100 mm beyond the heater. Set the rails parallel on the floor, spaced as far apart as the height of the stones in the heater. Cut seven 45 by 22 mm fence posts and nail them across the rails, one at each end and the rest spaced evenly between. Build a similar but narrower panel for the side of the heater. Nail a 45 by 45 mm post vertically to each wall just inside the point where the fence will attach. Nail each of the fence panels to a post and butt nail the free ends of the rails together at the corner where they meet.

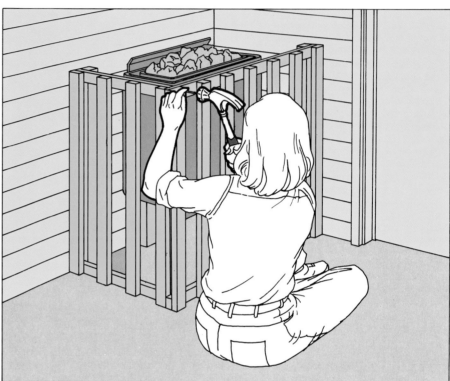

Correct Ventilation

Positioning the air vents. To maintain even distribution of heat inside the sauna, two air vents, an inlet and an outlet, are strategically positioned on the walls. The inlet is cut into the wall behind or next to the heater, about 150 mm above the floor, while the outlet is fitted high up on the wall, about 100 mm from the ceiling, as far away from the heater as possible. The vents should open on to the same well-ventilated indoor area. Otherwise differences in temperature could force the air flow to be reversed causing dangerously hot areas to build up on benches, floors and walls. For a family-sized sauna, both vents should be about 120 by 100 mm. Although the outlet may be fitted with a movable hatch to block off up to half of its opening, the inlet must always be completely open.

The position of the door in relation to the heater and vents is also important. Because it lets in cold air whenever it is opened, the door should ideally be sited on the same wall as the heater and inlet vent. Alternatively, they should be positioned close together on adjacent walls.

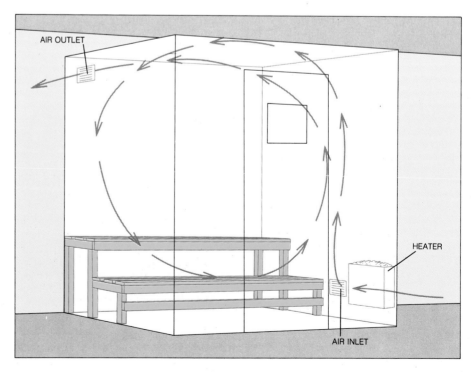

AIR OUTLET

HEATER

AIR INLET

Built-Ins for the Bath

A few tricks with wood can make a bathroom more convenient and appealing. By boxing in an old-fashioned claw-footed bath, you can give it a modern look. By adding a cabinet extension to fill the space between the end of the bath and a wall, you gain extra storage capacity as well as a convenient bath-level surface to hold toiletries, towels or even plants. The right wood, correctly installed, will easily survive the bathroom's damp environment.

Building additions like these involves mostly routine carpentry plus some special attention to fastening and fitting. Wood additions to bathroom fixtures must be firmly anchored to the floor or the wall since there is no easy way to attach wood to the rim of a bath or a basin. Nailing or screwing through ceramic tiles, the material most likely to be encountered in a bathroom *(right)*, requires only a little extra care in drilling holes through the brittle tiles. The wood should fit snugly to the fixture and careful caulking is essential wherever wood meets a wall, the floor or the edges of fixtures, to keep water from seeping in behind the wood structure.

Use exterior or marine-type plywood. Treat all exposed surfaces with one of the standard wood preservatives. For most sheathing 6 mm plywood will do but use 18 mm for any structures that are likely to bear much weight. After a framework has been attached and sheathed, it can be painted or covered with tiles, plastic laminate or carpet to match its surroundings.

Enclosing a Bath

1 **Building the frames.** Nail together a frame of 100 by 50 mm pieces of timber like that below for each side of the bath that is to be covered. Space the interior vertical studs of the frame about 400 mm apart. In designing the frame to fit under the lip of a lipped bath, or flush with the top of a non-lipped bath, allow for the thickness of 12 mm plywood round the top of the frame *(page 68, Step 3)* and of any finishing material for the top surface of the frame.

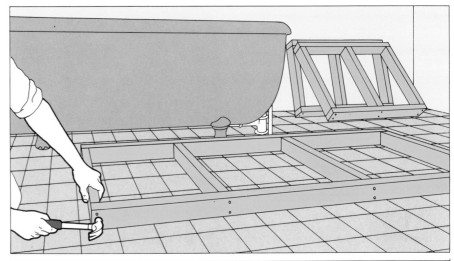

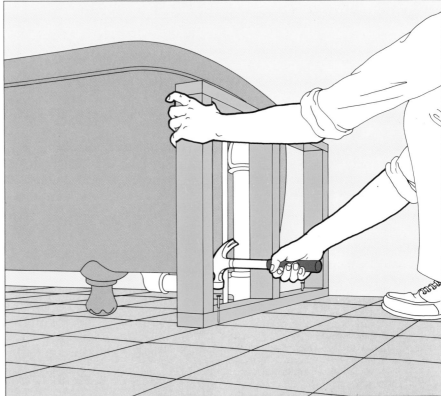

2 **Attaching the frames.** Drive 75 mm round-wire nails barely through the bottom of the frame in the middle of each space between studs. Set the frame in place and check for level. Tap each nail enough to nick the tile beneath. Remove the frame and drill through the tiles at each mark with a carbide-tipped bit slightly larger than the nails. Run silicone seal along the bottom outside edge of the frame, reposition it, and nail it to the floor through the tile holes. At corners, nail the end braces together. Where an end brace meets a wall, attach it with screws and wallplugs; on a timber frame wall, nail directly into a stud or use hollow-wall fixings.

3 **Attaching the top plywood.** Cover the top surface of the frame with 12 mm plywood nailed to the top members of the frame. These top pieces should fit under the lip of a lipped bath with room to spare for the finished surface.

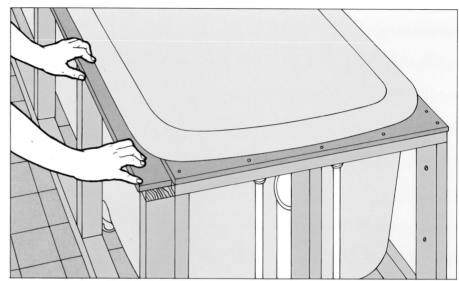

4 **Covering the frame.** Sheathe the outer sides of the frame with 6 mm plywood fastened with galvanized nails. Leave a 3 mm space as an expansion joint where the edges of the sheathing meet the floor or a wall. If you cover the sheathing and the top with plastic laminate, use the techniques illustrated on pages 30–35; if with ceramic tiles, those on pages 22–28. Caulk along the lines where the bath lip or rim meets the finished top surface of the frame or where the top meets the rim of a non-lipped bath.

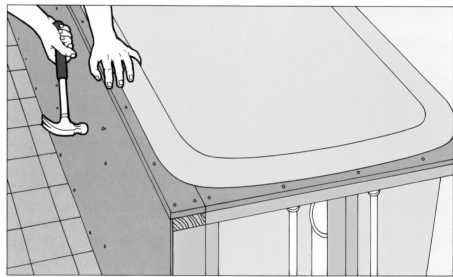

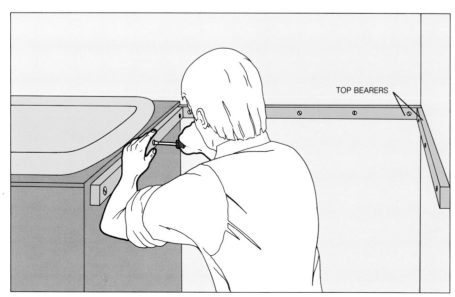

TOP BEARERS

Building a Cabinet Extension

1 **Making the top framework.** To position the cabinet top bearers, measure 12 mm below the top of the bath panelling and draw a guideline round the walls and the end of the bath panelling at this height. Check that the line is horizontal with a spirit level. Cut a length of 50 by 25 mm timber to fit between the bath panelling and the end wall; position the upper edge of this bearer on the guideline and screw it to the wall. Cut two 50 by 25 mm side bearers 50 mm shorter than the full cabinet depth, and screw these to the side wall and to the bath panelling (*left*).

2 **Finishing the cabinet top.** Screw a fourth 50 by 25 mm bearer to the front ends of the side bearers; if the width of the cabinet is greater than 500 mm, nail a centre bearer to the back and front bearers. Cut a piece of 12 mm exterior grade plywood to fit exactly on top of the framework, and nail it to the bearers with 25 mm panel pins or lost-head nails.

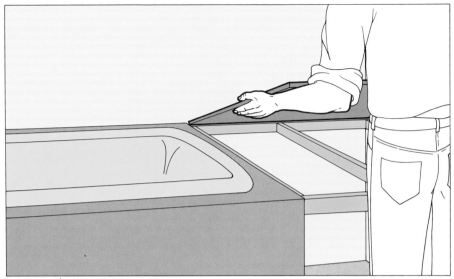

3 **Making the cabinet base.** Measure and cut two 75 by 25 mm pieces of timber to fit between the bottom of the bath panelling and the end wall; screw one of the pieces to the back wall at floor level, using a spirit level to check that it is horizontal. Cut three more 75 by 25 mm base supports 100 mm shorter than the full cabinet depth; check for level, then screw the side supports to the bath panelling and to the end wall, and toenail the centre support to the back support. Nail the front support to the ends of the centre and side supports *(left)*. Measure and cut an 18 mm plywood sheet for the bottom of the cabinet. Nail this to the supports with 37 mm oval or lost-head nails; the front of the plywood should overhang the front support by 50 mm.

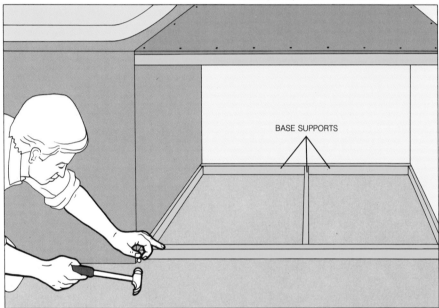

BASE SUPPORTS

4 **Installing the cabinet doors.** To make side linings, measure and cut two lengths of 75 by 25 mm timber to fit on either side of the cabinet between the base and the top frame. Measure and cut two 18 mm plywood doors to fit the front of the cabinet and hang them on the side linings with 63 mm steel or brass butt hinges *(left)*. Nail two short strips of wood to the cabinet frame, top and bottom, 20 mm in from the front, to act as door stops. Attach magnetic catches to the top of the cabinet doors and fix suitable handles.

Finish the top of the cabinet with tiles or plastic laminate to match the top surface of the bath panelling, and the cabinet front and doors with gloss paint. Apply sealant round all the cabinet edges which are adjacent to the walls, the floor and the bath panelling.

SIDE LINING

Professional Techniques for Hanging Mirrors

Mirrors must be handled with care because they are heavy, awkward and fragile. When fixing a mirror to the wall with screws or clips, always have a helper to support the glass while you mark the positions for holes and fixings. If the wall is not completely flat, set small adhesive-backed pads, available at glass shops, behind the mirror to space it away from the wall; this small space allows for the evaporation of trapped moisture. Tighten screws just enough to secure the mirror—overtightening will crack the glass.

Mirrors with predrilled holes near to the corners are attached to the wall by the use of special mirror screws (*opposite page, above*). Mirrors without holes are attached with clips, which are available in a variety of designs (*opposite page, below*). Drilling holes in a mirror is a difficult task, and is best left to a glazier. Small mirrors can also be attached with adhesive, but this installation is permanent because the mirrors usually break during any attempted removal. Mirrors that are backed with hardboard usually have steel hangers riveted to the backing which are simply slipped over flat hooks screwed into the wall.

On solid brick or masonry walls, drill holes and insert wallplugs to hold the fastening screws. On timber-frame walls, screw directly into the studs if possible; use hollow-wall fixings such as toggle bolts if the studs are not located conveniently. If the wall is faced with ceramic tiles, use a masonry drill bit to drill through the tiles and into the wall behind.

Carrying a mirror. Carry a mirror vertically, never horizontally; you can support and manoeuvre it more easily and it will not tend to crack under its own weight. Keep your feet and legs out from under the mirror in case it falls—and if it does slip from your grasp, get out of the way quickly. Protect your hands with cloth pads if the mirror edges are not ground smooth. Never attempt to catch a falling mirror.

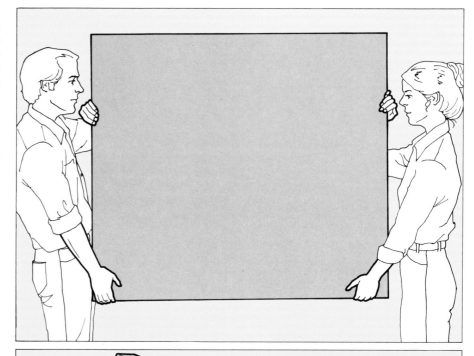

Checking the wall. Before hanging a mirror, slide a straight board or level, longer than the mirror is wide, around the wall to see if it wobbles on a high spot. If the wall is bowed or has irregularities of more than 3 mm, pack two or more adhesive-backed felt or rubber pads behind the mirror, which will keep it from coming into contact with the high spots.

Fixing a mirror with mirror screws. Get a helper to support the mirror against the wall where you intend to fix it. Check that the mirror is horizontal with a spirit level, then mark the wall with a pencil through each of the predrilled holes. Remove the mirror, drill holes at the marked positions and insert wallplugs. Get your helper to support the mirror while you secure the screws *(inset)*: at each hole in the mirror, place a spacer washer behind the mirror and then insert the mirror screw with its soft cup washer. Tighten the screws only until the cup washers press against the mirror; further pressure might crack the glass. Finally, screw the domehead covers into the threaded heads of the mirror screws.

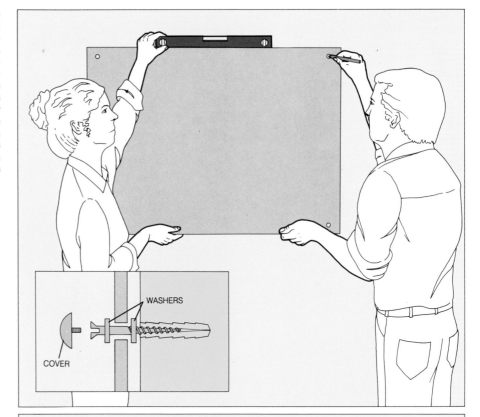

WASHERS

COVER

Attaching a mirror with clips. Using a spirit level, mark a horizontal guideline as wide as the mirror for the bottom. J-clips should be positioned about one-third of the width of the mirror in from the edges. Hold the bottom clips on the guideline and mark the positions for holes; drill the holes, insert wallplugs, then attach the clips with the screws and plastic washers provided. Support the mirror on the bottom clips and draw a line along the top. Remove the mirror, position the slotted top clips on the guideline directly above the bottom ones and attach them in the same way. Slide the top clips upwards, replace the mirror in the bottom clips, then push the top clips down to secure the mirror.

   Corner clips *(inset)* are positioned and fixed to the wall in much the same way as J-clips. Secure the bottom clips first, then insert the mirror and attach the top clips.

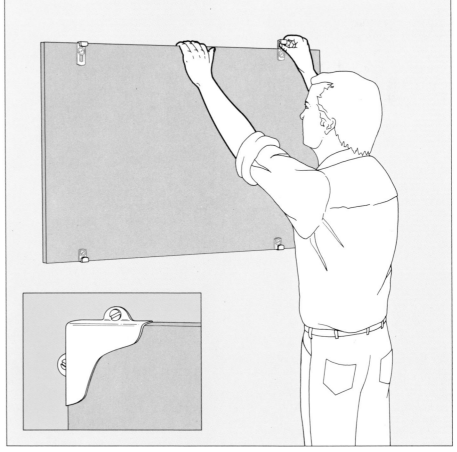

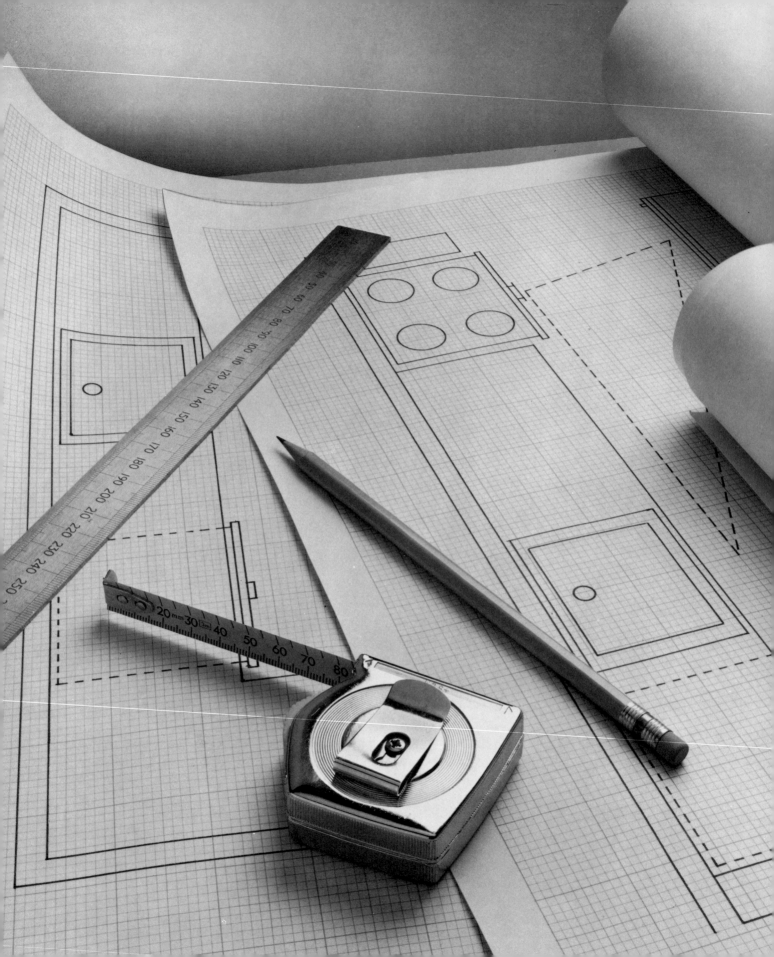

3 Planning for the Big Job

Tools for planning. Alternative floor plans for a new kitchen illustrate proposed sites for the principal units and appliances. The plans are drawn to scale on graph paper from actual measurements made with a measuring tape. The most efficient layout for the family cook is determined by calculating the distance between the three main activity centres—cooker, refrigerator and sink (pages 78–81).

Nobody invented the modern kitchen and bathroom. Both rooms just grew over the past century and a half as manufacturers began to mass produce the devices that make them functional: cookers, sinks, refrigerators, showers. Some of these essential fixtures—the bath and W.C., for instance—were ancient but so rare that ordinary people did not even know of their existence; others, like the microwave oven, are products of space-age technology. New or old, the operation of the fixtures has proved to be less of a problem than the task of arranging them within a room. Where you place cooker and sink, refrigerator and dishwasher, bath and vanity unit may have more effect on the usefulness, convenience and attractiveness of a kitchen or bathroom than the design of the fixtures themselves. As a result, planning the job, whether you are remodelling an existing room or building an entirely new one, is as important as the mechanics of installing pipes and appliances.

While minor improvements in layout can be made whenever fixtures are changed, the best opportunity comes when you undertake major remodelling or start to build a kitchen or bathroom where none existed before. Then you can take advantage of research showing how to minimize the cook's work in a kitchen and of practical experience showing how to place fixtures to minimize the work involved in running pipes.

But while this background of knowledge may suggest an ideal layout, other factors may limit your ability to achieve the ideal. One is cost, of course; almost any layout desired is possible in a big room, but space is expensive and therefore often scarce in more modern homes. Another obstacle is legal—the various codes that regulate plumbing, wiring and house structure. But the house itself usually exerts the greatest influence on what you can do; existing plumbing and walls largely determine where fixtures can be placed and where new kitchens and bathrooms can be constructed, and unless you adapt your plans to the structure you have, remodelling or adding becomes almost as big a job as building an entirely new house.

For most people, the first problem to be faced is space. Generally, there is too little to provide for all desired uses. But in some old houses, there is so much that it may be wasted or distributed inconveniently. In both cases, different solutions apply to kitchen and bathroom.

The big bathroom is generally easy to improve by subdividing it (page 85). The small bathroom suffers severe restrictions imposed by the sizes of fixtures. The minimum space for a full bathroom containing a standard bath, W.C. and washbasin is 1800 by 1400 mm, but even in this minimum, a number of layouts are possible (pages 82–84). And bathrooms can be fitted into smaller areas by using space-saving fixtures. A 1070 by 710 mm "sit-up" bath takes up less than 0.77 square metres of floor space, compared to 1.19 square metres for the standard 1700 by 700 mm model. With a small or corner-mounted washbasin and a W.C. with a short projection pan and a slimline cistern, you can squeeze a cloakroom into a total area of 1.5 square metres.

Space-saving appliances are also available for small kitchens. There are refrigerators only 545 mm high by 380 mm wide by 405 mm deep, and miniature ovens 330 mm high by 550 mm wide by 350 mm deep that can be wall-hung or put on a work surface; and sinks that fit cut-outs of only 444 by 429 mm. Such devices are often indispensable in the kitchens of studios and tiny flats, but the kitchens of most homes require full-sized appliances, and the planning focuses on arranging them for maximum convenience while still providing space for all the other purposes the room must serve—as a place for family dining, homework and socializing.

Some solutions to these problems have been devised through research carried out after World War II, principally at Cornell University in the U.S.A., which subjected the housewife's chores to the detailed time and motion studies previously applied to factory work. By filming women preparing meals, researchers discovered that as many as 252 trips to the refrigerator, the sink, the cooker and the work surface were needed to prepare dinner; just to throw together breakfast in some households took over 40 such trips. The researchers also found that more trips were made between sink and cooker than between refrigerator and work surface. The conclusions were obvious. Arranging the appliances so that they lie in a work triangle within easy reach of one another—sink and cooker or hob closest to each other—and removing obstacles such as kitchen tables in the path between them results in faster, less tiring kitchen work. These findings have provided the basis for the layout of almost all kitchens today, and in 1961 the Parker Morris Report in the U.K. confirmed the value of setting the sink and hob close to each other by recommending a sequence of work surface/hob/work surface/sink/work surface in a continuous run.

The Cornell studies also showed that in the average kitchen, the cook is alone for only 50 per cent of the time, establishing that even modern "efficient" kitchens are more than simply food-preparation centres. By applying these results as shown on pages 79–81, you can design almost any kitchen to take full advantage of all the available space—gaining both a streamlined work area and sufficient room for informal dining and for family gatherings.

While efficiency research and fixture designs suggest ideal plans for kitchen and bathroom, the realities of house structure and legal codes and regulations determine what is feasible. If your present kitchen is very small, or has a large number of doors and windows, some structural work may facilitate a more efficient kitchen. For instance, blocking up or moving a window or door could give you a better flow of units and appliances; and the same logic applies to bathrooms. Plumbing is yet another consideration and is often the major limitation in bathrooms. Most houses have at least one plumbing stack (*pages 76–77*)—a modern house will usually have only one—a "tree" of branching pipes along which all fixtures of kitchen, bath and laundry are strung, taking their water supplies from its small pipes and emptying their waste into its large ones. Any changes you plan should take into account the existing stack, for adding new branches to it is easier than installing an entirely new tree. A new stack is often practical, however, particularly if the house has rooms or cupboards that provide space for hiding large pipes.

How the fixtures can be set along a stack, new or old, is spelled out in the several codes of practice listed in the building regulations that govern all construction. Nearly all codes permit amateurs to do most (but not necessarily all) of the work on their own homes, providing they get approval and arrange for inspections. In Australia and New Zealand, however, all plumbing, wiring and gas fittings may be done only by a licensed professional. Although code requirements vary from place to place, they are generally based on a sound rationale. By requiring techniques and materials that suit local needs, they guide you towards a safe and durable job.

The building regulations also control structural alterations. In most areas, for instance, you must obtain approval to remove a load-bearing wall or to tamper with an exterior wall—whether building an addition or simply adding a new window or blocking off an old door—or to re-route underground drainage or reposition a vent stack. Some codes also require approval for less complex work, such as adding or removing a non-loadbearing partition wall or for altering the use of a room. Of particular concern when remodelling a kitchen or bathroom are those regulations concerning plumbing and wiring, heating flues and ventilation.

Unless you are already familiar with the building regulations and local codes of practice—copies are available through the local authority's planning department or at local libraries—contact your local authority building control officer before you commence work; he may be attached to the planning department of the local council or to the borough engineer's department. Initially, the best approach is to show the building control officer your rough plans so that you have a basis for discussion. You need not, at this stage, submit elaborate plans; but they should be drawn to scale, and comprise an "existing" plan and a "proposed" plan, with the location of walls (stating whether they are load-bearing), doors and windows accurately indicated. In addition, the essential plumbing, electrical and heating systems should be clearly marked.

The building control officer will then inform you whether the proposed work is affected by the building regulations. Depending on these regulations, you may require approval—whether from the council, or landlord or neighbours. In addition, you may also require planning permission. An application for planning permission entails submitting a form, along with your proposed plans, and payment of a small fee.

Depending on whether you require approval and planning permission, the building control officer will then advise whether the plans need to be drawn in greater detail. You may also need additional copies of your plans for approval from the fire authority and from the electricity and gas boards.

Often, the detailed information required from the plan is complex, and unless this information is conveyed sufficiently well, your proposals may be rejected. It may, therefore, be advisable to have the plans drawn by a professional architect or draughtsman. Once you have submitted your drawings, and obtained the necessary approvals, you, or your builder, can proceed with the work. Inspections are made by the building control officer while work is in progress and upon completion.

Finding the Best Pathways for the Piping

Remodelling a kitchen or bathroom; or installing a new one, is a major job that requires major planning. Before you turn the first screw or hammer the first nail, you must make basic decisions about the sizes and styles of fixtures and appliances, clearances, floor and wall coverings, lighting, heating and ventilation. Most important of all, you must decide upon the routes of new plumbing lines *(right)*. The location of existing plumbing and the distance it can be moved—if at all—will often dictate the layout of a remodelled kitchen or bathroom, and it may also limit your choice of a new location. As an added precaution, check the plans with your local water authority.

In most homes, plumbing fixtures are clustered around a core of supply pipes and waste pipes. A bathroom is often located above or behind the kitchen. In an indirect supply system—as shown in the illustration opposite—the cold water storage cistern supplies all the cold water taps and appliances except the kitchen cold tap, which is connected to the mains; in a direct supply system, the cold water storage cistern supplies only the hot water cylinder, and all cold water taps and appliances are supplied under mains pressure. In Australia and New Zealand, however, the hot water supply system is often supplied under direct mains pressure as well.

Used water and sewage are carried away from the fixtures by branch wastes that run to large vertical pipes known as stacks, dropping down to the main house drain, or sewer. In a two stack system, used water runs into the waste stack and sewage into the soil stack; in a single stack system—as shown opposite—both empty into the same pipe. Each fixture has a trap seal that prevents sewer gases from entering the house. In addition, the waste and soil stacks extend one metre above the eaves as vent pipes that emit waste gases and admit fresh air, maintaining atmospheric pressure behind the flow of drain water and wastes, and thus preventing water from being siphoned out of the traps.

Installing plumbing where none exists involves running new piping through the walls, floors and ceilings. Waste and soil pipes must be planned and installed *(pages 102–107)* before the supply lines. Wastes work by gravity: they are large (32 to 106 mm in diameter), and must be pitched on horizontal runs and kept as straight as possible. The location of waste pipes is rigidly governed by plumbing codes. If their location exceeds a specified "critical distance" from an existing vent *(page 106)*, you must install a new vent.

Extending supply pipes usually poses fewer problems. They are relatively small (15 to 22 mm in diameter) and can be elbowed into sharp turns. But added fixtures can reduce the water flow through the supply lines in a system that already has low pressure or constricted pipes. If you have either of these problems, investigate possible remedies *(pages 113–115)* before planning any plumbing additions.

Concealing new pipes, especially the large waste pipes, can be tricky. If the new kitchen or bathroom is over accessible floorboards and joists, horizontal pipes can be run beneath the floor. The pipe's passage is achieved by cutting a series of notches in the uppermost side—never the underside—of the joists. For a new installation above a finished ceiling, you may have to cut away part of the ceiling to install the pipes; and you may have to drill or notch the joists of the floor—or attic—above. There are limits on where and how deeply you can cut a joist. For instance, to avoid unnecessary weakening of the joists at their most vulnerable stress point, you should cut the pathway of notches along one side of the joists rather than through the middle. And you must not cut a notch deeper than one fifth of the joist's depth *(page 94)*. Because of such limitations, you may have to run the pipes over a floor, or below a ceiling, then box them in.

Vertical pipes can be concealed inside a framed structure called a wet wall, which is substantially thicker than an ordinary partition and created by furring out an existing wall *(page 94)* or building an entirely new one *(pages 96–97)*. Alternatively, pipes can be run alongside an existing wall and concealed—in cabinets, bookcases, cupboards or specially made panelling.

To facilitate cleaning, horizontal pipes not being concealed should be installed at least 100 mm above floor level. To prevent unnecessary heat loss, avoid running pipes along the inside of exterior walls.

Electricity routes for a new bathroom or kitchen can pose fewer problems than new plumbing routes. Electric cable is flexible and can easily be snaked through hollow walls and ceilings or run through surface conduits; alternatively, channels can be cut into brick or blockwork to accommodate it. The new lines can be powered from existing socket outlets or directly from the consumer unit. Ducts are bulkier, but usually not difficult to run: the fans for bathrooms or kitchen cooker hoods *(pages 52–55)* are usually vented through lengths of duct which run to the outside through the sides of the house.

Since plumbing pipes, electric cables and vent ducts may have to run over long distances, route them in the same direction if you can, to minimize the cutting and patching of walls and ceilings. This part of the planning job is tricky. For example, if you plan to expand a room by removing a wall *(pages 92–93)*, be sure that you will not endanger the house structure or disrupt any of the vital services.

First determine whether the wall is load-bearing *(page 92)*—all outside walls of houses are. Then find out what services the wall contains. Electric switches or socket outlets indicate wiring that must be removed or relocated. Heating outlet grilles indicate ducts, which can be rerouted but generally not removed. Ducts that cannot be rerouted must be left in place and boxed in with panelling.

The presence of plumbing fixtures along a wall, or along a corresponding wall in the room directly above, may indicate pipes within the wall that must be moved. If the plumbing ends at the existing fixtures, it can be removed and capped *(page 91)*. Supply pipes and branch waste pipes passing through the wall to fixtures above can usually be rerouted. But soil stacks—more difficult to reroute—are usually left in place and concealed.

Once you know where you can best place the new services, make a floor plan of the room, indicating the locations and dimensions for walls, doors, windows, and plumbing and electrical outlets. Follow the plan as closely as you can in every step of the remodelling process, from running plumbing and electrical routes to arranging fixtures and appliances—and even to ordering and cutting new wall and floor coverings.

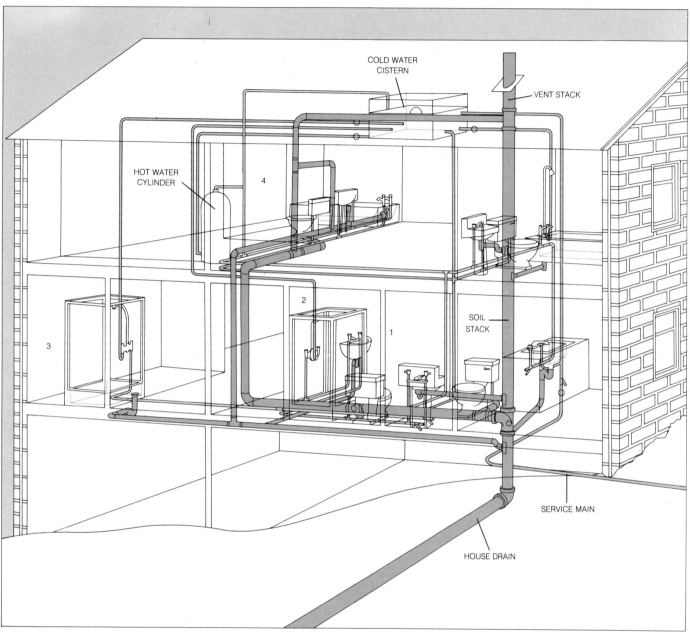

COLD WATER
CISTERN

VENT STACK

HOT WATER
CYLINDER

4

2

1

3

SOIL
STACK

SERVICE MAIN

HOUSE DRAIN

Paths for new pipes. In this house, the existing plumbing core consists of two systems of pipes installed for a ground-floor kitchen and a first-floor bathroom immediately above it. Soil and waste pipes and vents *(grey)* run to a combined waste and soil stack that vents gases through the roof and carries waste products down to the main drain. In the indirect system of supply pipes *(orange and beige)* cold water taps (except the kitchen tap) and appliances are supplied from the cold water storage cistern, and hot water taps are supplied via the hot water cylinder.

Four new installations—a W.C. and basin in the small room next to the kitchen, a shower room and a second separate shower on the ground floor, and a full bathroom on the first floor—illustrate ways in which new plumbing can be added to an existing system.

1. W.C. The waste from the basin is connected directly to the soil stack, and that from the W.C. enters the soil pipe extension from the new first-floor bathroom. Hot and cold water are supplied via new connections from the existing first-floor bathroom supplies.

2. Shower room. The W.C. is connected to the soil pipe from the new first-floor bathroom; the shower waste is connected to the new waste from the separate shower. Cold water for the shower is supplied through a new pipe leading directly from the cold water storage cistern; all other cold and hot water supplies are fed through extensions from the vertical pipes supplying other new ground-floor installations.

3. Separate shower. The shower is connected to the soil stack by a long horizontal waste pipe from which a vent leads up to connect with that from the new first-floor bathroom. Cold water is supplied directly from the cold water storage cistern; hot water is supplied through an extension from the pipe feeding the new shower room.

4. First-floor bathroom. The W.C. waste leads down to the new shower room and on to the soil stack, and is vented through a new pipe that joins the existing vent just before it exits from the roof. The waste from the bath and basin leads down to connect with the waste from the separate shower, and is connected to the new vent pipe. Cold water is supplied through a new pipe teed off from the vertical pipe supplying the existing bathroom and the new ground-floor installations; hot water is supplied from the hot water cylinder.

Basing a Kitchen on a Step-Saving Triangle

It has been estimated that a family cook walks about 250 kilometres during the course of preparing a year's meals. As much as a third of this marathon performance may be unnecessary, inflicted upon the cook by appliances placed not for efficiency but for economy in construction.

An efficient kitchen will have its major fixtures and appliances in one of the four basic layouts shown on pages 80–81: the U, the L, the double-galley and the single-galley. In each layout, the lines joining the three activity centres—the refrigerator, the sink and the hob—form what is known as the work triangle. The perfect work triangle keeps distances between the refrigerator, sink and hob as short as possible, yet provides adequate working and storage space. With good planning, the sides of the triangle measure between 3600 and 6600 mm. Avoid any layouts that route household traffic through the work triangle; between base units or appliances that face each other allow a distance of 1200 to 1800 mm—enough space to enable you to stand at an open base unit or appliance while another person edges past.

The sink is the main activity centre, accounting for 40 to 46 per cent of all kitchen work time. Ideally it belongs at the centre of the work triangle, within 1200 to 1800 mm of the hob, and within 1200 to 2100 mm of the refrigerator. Locate the dishwasher within 300 mm of the sink, for convenient loading and the simplest pattern of plumbing connections, but do not set the dishwasher at right angles to the sink, or you will have to move away from the sink every time you want to open the dishwasher door. Bear in mind that dishwashers, washing machines and tumbledriers will need to be pulled in and out of position for servicing, so they require adequate clearance for this: for a standard-size 600 mm-deep appliance, allow 650 mm.

A single-bowl sink, or a 1½-bowl sink, is adequate for a kitchen with a dishwasher; use a double-bowl model if you plan to wash and rinse dishes by hand. To provide space for the cleaning of large oven trays and pans, choose a sink with a bowl that measures at least 500 by 350 by 175 mm.

The hob is the cooking and serving centre, and is best located for easy access to the dining area. It is also the spot at which most kitchen injuries occur. Always avoid an arrangement in which people passing through the kitchen are likely to brush against the hob, and never place a hob under a window: curtains can blaze up easily, and you must reach across the burners to open and close the window.

On either side of the hob, the worktop should have heat-resistant areas for hot pots and pans. These areas can be commercial "worktop savers"—usually made of reinforced glass—that are incorporated into a worktop cutout. A cooker hood for extracting cooking odours, grease and steam must be installed at least 600 mm above an electric hob and 700 mm above a gas hob, *(pages 52–55)*. Wall units placed over the hob should be at least 750 mm above the cooking rings.

The hob and the oven may be combined in a single, freestanding cooker unit, but the modern trend is for a split arrangement: a built-in hob and a separate built-in oven that is wall-mounted at a convenient height for the cook—and out of the reach of small children. An oven is the least used of all major kitchen appliances—it accounts for less than 10 per cent of the trips to and from the activity centre—so it can lie outside the work triangle without a significant loss of efficiency. The bottom of a wall oven should be 75 mm below elbow height, a level that minimizes the chance of burning an arm on an oven rack and is comfortable for turning or basting food. Separate ovens and hobs usually require more space than a single cooker unit, but even in a small kitchen you can achieve a split arrangement by installing a built-under oven which can be fitted beneath either a worktop or a special slimline hob.

Locate the refrigerator or fridge-freezer at the end of a worktop, where it will not cut the available work space into several small, cramped work areas. Choose a refrigerator with hinges away from the counter, so that the open door will not block work space—many modern models have doors adjustable to open either way. This criterion does not necessarily apply to built-under refrigerators, which can be placed beneath the worktop.

The design and installation requirements of refrigerators vary considerably; follow manufacturers' instructions carefully. Built-in refrigerators are designed to be contained within a tall housing unit. Freestanding refrigerators, on the other hand, require ventilation, and must not be enclosed. Set these models at least 75 mm from the rear wall, so that heat from the condenser coils at the back of the refrigerator can disperse. Allow 25 to 50 mm between each side of the refrigerator and an adjacent unit, or wall; and do not obstruct the ventilation grille which is sited at the back of the top panel.

Any of the three activity centres can be located in a kitchen island or peninsula, but islands are seldom practical in average kitchens because they require at least 1500 mm of floor space on one of their long sides and at least 900 mm along their short ones. Even if you have adequate floor space for an island, avoid using it for the hob or the main sink: both of these centres need more worktop than most island installations permit.

In practice, the worktop area for an activity centre may vary considerably from the dimensions recommended in the plans opposite and at the top of page 80. In a limited space two activity centres can share a worktop area, but try to keep a shared worktop at least as long as the most generous minimum length for the two centres, plus 300 mm. And at some point in the assembly (usually between the refrigerator and sink) try to keep at least a 1000 mm length of worktop for a mixing and food-preparation centre.

The standard kitchen worktop measures 900 mm in height and 600 mm from front to back. Some expensive base units are available in a range of heights, enabling you to adapt the worktop height to the level you find most convenient to work at; alternatively, the height of standard base units can usually be adjusted by raising or lowering the plinth *(page 47)*. If you wish to install a worktop deeper than 600 mm, to provide extra storage space along the back while still allowing adequate room for food preparation, you can build out the wall with timber spacers, against which standard-size base units can be secured in a forward position.

A large kitchen permits more variations, but has one paradoxical limitation: try not to exceed the maximum recommended dimensions of the plans. Extra work space means extra steps between the centres—and extra work for the cook.

The Three Activity Centres

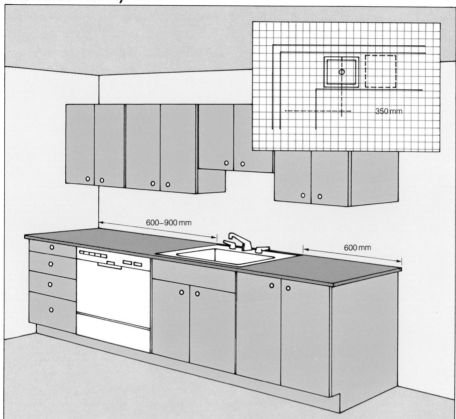

The sink. Provide at least 600 mm of worktop on each side of the sink for preparing food and stacking dishes. If the worktop surface on one side is in the form of a ridged drainer, the worktop on the other side of the sink should be at least 900 mm long; if ridged drainers are set on both sides of the sink, an additional worktop length of 600 mm will be needed for food preparation. For a sink which is placed near a corner *(inset)*, allow at least 350 mm between the sink centre line and the corner.

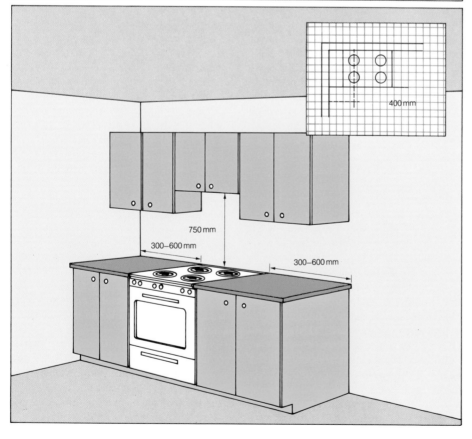

The hob. Allow at least 300 mm of worktop on each side of the hob for resting pans, or up to 600 mm on each side if space permits. For a hob next to a wall *(inset)*, allow a safety margin of at least 400 mm from the centre of the nearest burner. If the oven is a separate unit, there should be a worktop at least 400 mm long beside it. If the cooking zone also functions as a serving zone, an unbroken run of worktop at least 600 mm long will be required for setting out dishes. Wall units situated directly above a hob must be mounted at least 750 mm above the rings or burners.

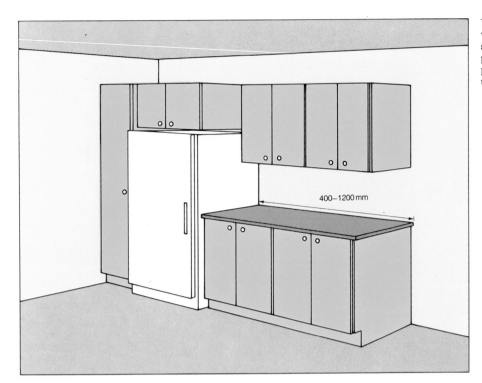

The retrigerator centre. Provide at least 400 mm of worktop on the latch side of the refrigerator for setting out supplies. If this area must also form part of the mixing and food preparation centre, provide an uninterrupted run of worktop between 900 and 1200 mm long.

400–1200 mm

The Four Layouts

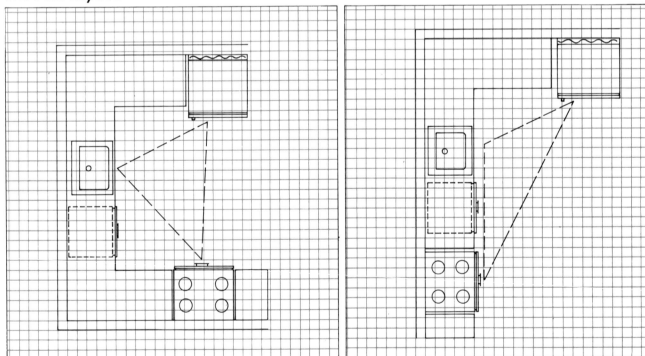

The U. Units and worktops set along three walls keep the three activity centres accessible to one another and out of the way of other traffic. The back wall should measure between 2400 and 4000 mm, allowing from 1200 to 2800 mm of work area between worktops—a tighter arrangement makes for cramped work areas; a looser one, too many steps between activity centres.

The L. This adaptable plan is best for small square kitchens; in large ones it provides a work triangle isolated from traffic and frees the rest of the room for dining. Its main drawback is the long distance between two of the work centres. Arrange the centres with a sink in the middle, creating a refrigerator-to-sink-to-hob work flow.

The double-galley. In this arrangement, usually found in a kitchen that also serves as a passageway, appliances and units are distributed along two facing walls. Because the work triangle will be broken by traffic, try to locate the hob and the sink—the most active work centres—along the same wall. The aisle should be at least 1200 mm wide to provide adequate clearance between unit and appliance doors. If your aisle is narrower, try to stagger the three work centres so that appliance doors do not interfere with one another.

The single-galley. This layout works best in an area less than 3660 mm long; if the arrangement is strung out to gain more units and longer worktops, the distances between work centres become too great for efficiency. Use narrow appliances to provide maximum worktop and unit space, and save steps by locating the refrigerator at one end, the hob at the other and the sink in between, with most of the worktop space situated between the sink and the hob.

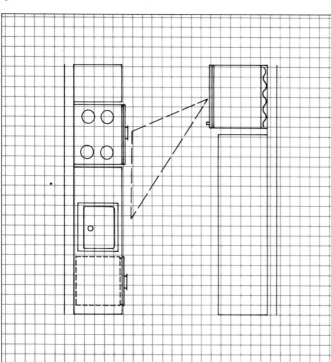

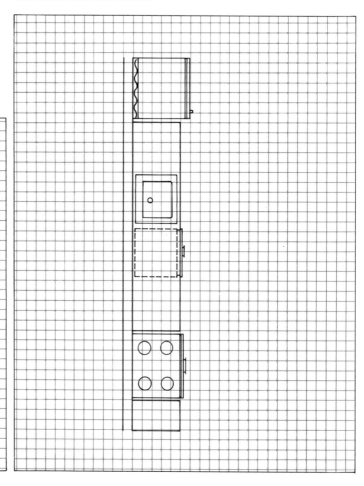

Making a Dangerous Room Safer

According to the Health and Safety Executive, about a quarter of all serious home accidents take place in the kitchen. The placement of appliances and the arrangement of work spaces shown on these pages reduce or eliminate many potential hazards, but designers and safety experts also recommend safety measures for specific danger points.

☐ Choose a kitchen hob that has controls placed at the front or sides, not at the back of the burners.

☐ Hang a dry chemical fire extinguisher designed for grease fires within easy reach of the hob—but do not hang it directly above the hob, where you might have to reach through flames for it.

☐ Hang kitchen doors so that they swing out of the room when opened, rather than into the work triangle.

☐ Locate hanging or wall-mounted light fixtures at least 2040 mm above the floor, unless they hang over an island, a base cabinet or a table.

☐ Install an adequate number of socket outlets, and site them as close as possible to the appliances they supply, to avoid trailing lengths of flex or cable.

☐ Socket outlets and switches, except those operated by a pull cord, should, if possible, not be within 900 mm of a sink. The switch for a sink waste-disposal unit should be located out of reach of children.

☐ Store sharp knives and implements and poisonous products in places that are inaccessible to children.

Bathrooms to Fit the Space

Bathrooms are usually the smallest rooms in a house—and even a large bathroom has a way of seeming inadequate when every member of the family wants to use it at the same time. You may be able to use the space more efficiently by adding a second washbasin or partitioning off a W.C.; in some situations, you can enlarge a bathroom by removing a wall and gaining extra space from an adjoining room or cupboard. But the most satisfactory solution to the problem is another bathroom—a new one, built into whatever space is available. A full bathroom with standard fixtures can fit into a space of 1800 by 1400 mm, a half bath, W.C. and sink into a space as small as 1400 by 900 mm.

In such small rooms, the fixtures must be placed with special care to provide minimum clearances at the front and sides—use the diagrams on the right as a guide. At the same time, the layout of the bathroom is influenced by the location of existing plumbing or the routes of new pipes. Juggling the positions of your bathroom fixtures to meet both requirements calls for ingenuity and patience.

Position the W.C. as close as possible to an existing soil stack. Try to locate the W.C. next to a wall, for convenience in mounting a toilet-paper holder, but remember that some people find the sight of a W.C. from an open door objectionable. If the space is available, consider separating the W.C. from the other fixtures in the bathroom with a partition.

For convenience in plumbing, baths should be located along a wall or in a corner: the pipework can be supported by the wall and concealed by the bath itself, and the bath waste can be led directly through the wall without having to pass across the floor. All baths must be positioned to provide easy access to the pipework for plumbing repairs; on many baths, the side panel can be removed to expose the pipes.

The basin is the most frequently used fixture. Where possible, place it well away from the bath and W.C., with space round it for towel racks and hooks, toothbrush racks and cabinets or storage shelves. In a windowed bathroom, try to give the basin the advantage of natural light for shaving and applying make-up.

The routes of the pipes to and from the fixtures require careful planning. The details of the routes will depend on the floor plan, the location of existing plumbing and the requirements of your local plumbing regulations. Three of the most common fixture arrangements, each one with progressively more complicated plumbing, are shown in the floor plans on the right and on page 84. The plans are for the smallest practical rooms, but the plumbing patterns will also serve large bathrooms and additional fixtures (page 85). If you plan to install a wet wall to conceal the pipework, first mark on the existing wall the dimensions, waste outlets and supply connections of the fixtures as guides for positioning the pipes (opposite page, above).

In any small bathroom, new or old, you will confront the problem of getting adequate storage and counter space. Some simple solutions:
□ Mount shallow shelves along a wall behind the door.
□ Install corner shelves in a free corner of the bathroom—these take up little space but can accommodate many toiletries and other bathroom accessories.
□ Set the hinges on the door so that it swings outwards when opened.
□ Replace a wall-mounted or pedestal basin with a vanity unit that provides both counter space and an enclosed cabinet beneath the basin.
□ Extend a vanity unit top over the top of the toilet cistern—use a removable extension, so that you can get to the cistern, if necessary, for repairs.
□ Use the space above the toilet cistern as a storage wall.

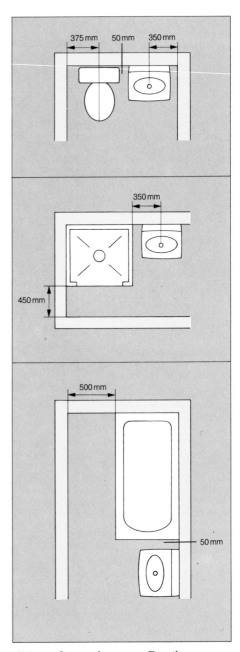

Minimum fixture clearances. For the average adult, the clearances indicated in the floor plans above are the minimums for using standard bathroom fixtures and cleaning round them. Minimum clearances mean minimal comfort: exceed the figures if you can. For example, a 350 mm clearance between the centre line of a basin and a wall, allows barely enough room to shave or apply make-up; 450 mm between a shower and a wall allows only enough room to edge out of the shower. When a W.C. and a basin or bath face each other, 450 mm between them provides no more than knee room in front of the W.C. and just enough room to stand in front of the basin or to dry oneself beside the bath. Most bathroom designers recommend 600 or 700 mm minimum clearances for comfortable use of these fixtures.

Rough-in dimensions. If you intend to conceal the pipework for new fixtures behind a wet wall (*pages 94–97*), make a template of the rear outline of each fixture and mark its dimensions on to the original wall surface. Mark the centre of each pipe hole precisely: this will enable you to align the pipework accurately with the fixture's supplies and waste. The wall marks on the right match the plumbing pattern shown below.

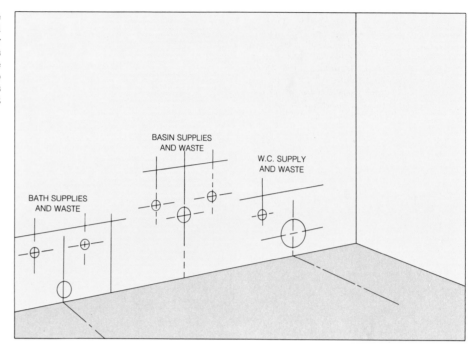

BASIN SUPPLIES
AND WASTE

W.C. SUPPLY
AND WASTE

BATH SUPPLIES
AND WASTE

Three Basic Plumbing Patterns

One wall. The simplest bathroom for a limited space has fixtures in a row, with all their plumbing along a single wall. This arrangement calls for the least amount of cutting into the house structure and uses the fewest fittings.

Where the basin and bath share a common waste—as in the arrangement here—the waste pipe diameter should be 50 mm and not 40 mm, to reduce the risk of siphoning the bath waste trap seal. To further protect the trap seal, install an anti-siphon device (*page 106*).

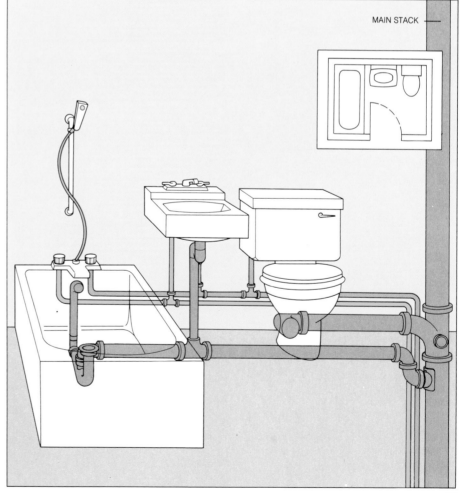

MAIN STACK

Two walls. A bathroom with plumbing on two adjoining walls provides somewhat more storage and activity space around the basin than a one-wall room, and the plumbing is only slightly more complicated. In the arrangement shown here, the bath waste is connected to a special soil tee that will accept both W.C. and bath discharge pipes. The basin waste is connected to the stack with a boss connection above the soil tee.

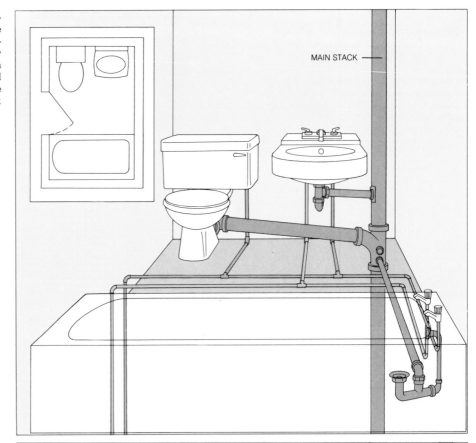

Three walls. Of all the basic bathroom plans, this offers the greatest flexibility and the largest wall and counter spaces—at the cost of added room area and more work in concealing the pipework. The room should be at least 1800 by 1400 mm to accommodate minimum clearances between fixtures; in practice, three-wall bathrooms are usually set up in larger rooms—at least 2300 by 1800 mm. In the room shown on the right, the basin and bath wastes are connected to the stack with boss connections made above and below the W.C. soil pipe entry.

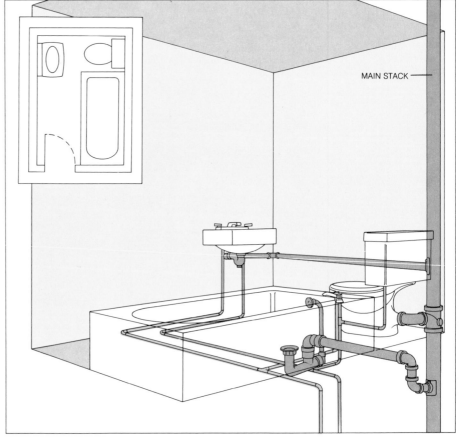

The Luxury That Size Allows

An expanded bathroom. Additional fixtures can be added to any of the basic bathroom plans with surprisingly little additional plumbing. For example, a 2100 by 1500 mm one-wall bathroom *(inset)* is here expanded with a second W.C. and a vanity unit, installed in what had been an adjoining storage room; the partition wall and interconnecting door are, of course, retained.

In the illustration shown below, the new W.C. is joined to the long horizontal soil pipe of the existing W.C., and the vanity unit basin waste is connected directly to the soil stack with a boss connector. Supply pipes for both the new W.C. and the vanity unit basin are teed off from the existing supply pipes.

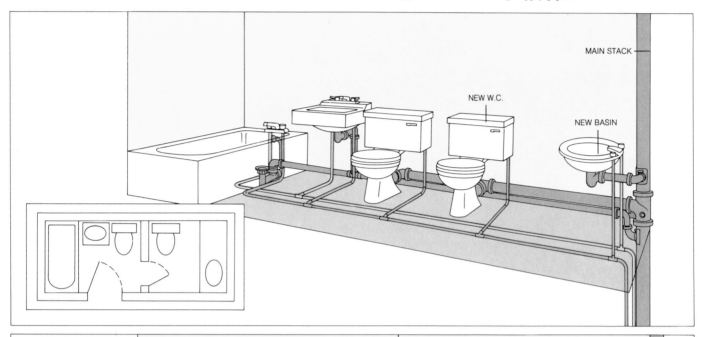

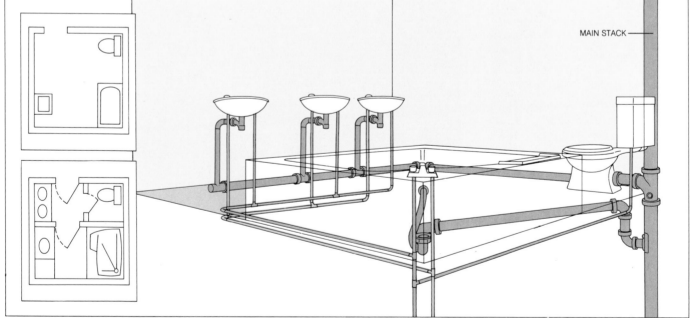

A redesigned bathroom. Many older homes have very large bathrooms that are equipped with no more than a standard bath, a W.C. and a basin. In a typical 3300 by 3000 mm room *(top inset)*, the remainder of the space is wasted. For maximum versatility, the room can be partitioned into functionally separate sections, with new doors between them *(bottom inset)*. The section nearest the original door becomes a powder room with a double-bowl vanity unit and an enclosed W.C. The inner section gets a new oversized bath, and a vanity unit and dressing table replace the old standing basin. The three basins are fed by pipes teed off from common supply pipes, which are themselves teed off from the bath supply pipes. The three basins also share a common 50 mm waste pipe; the bath waste is routed separately to the main soil stack.

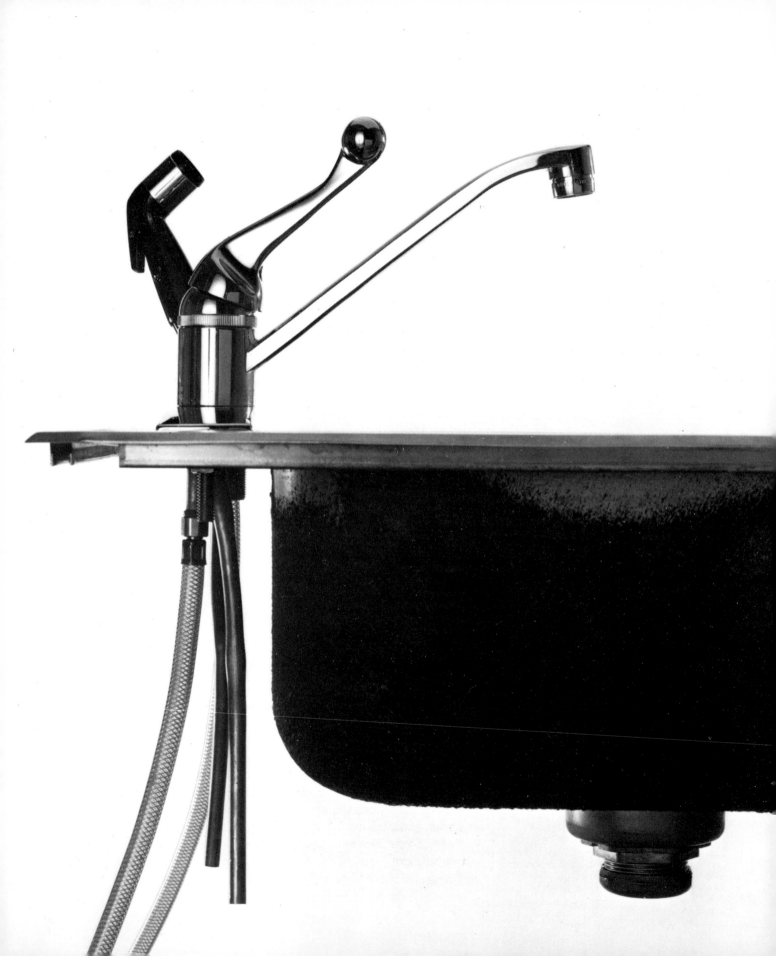

Plumbing for the New Rooms

Profile of a sink. Hidden beneath the gleam of the chrome fittings and stainless steel bowl are the unglamorous parts involved in the installation of a new sink. The rim is secured to the worktop with clamps. Extending down from the single-lever mixer tap assembly are copper tubes that are connected to the house supply lines with soldered or compression fittings. The hose of the spray attaches to the tap assembly, and the waste connection which is beneath the sink is made with a hexagon nut.

Creating a new kitchen or bathroom is an undertaking that can be less formidable than it seems at first. The trick is to reduce the procedures involved to the minimum necessary for your requirements. It may call for no more than the removal and replacement of old fixtures *(pages 88–91)* or, at a more ambitious level, the installation of new walls *(pages 96–99)*. Use as much of the existing plumbing as you can. Where extensions are necessary, choose materials that are easy to work with; you do not have to match new plumbing materials to old because adapters make the transition. The easiest is PVC, light in weight, readily cut with a hacksaw and assembled with push-fit or solvent-welded joints; it is now almost universally used for wastes and vents and in many areas cPVC is accepted for hot as well as cold supply lines.

While remodelling in most rooms of the house can proceed at a leisurely pace, kitchens and bathrooms require swift transitions to minimize the loss of their important functions. Have everything you need on hand before you begin. Do not rely on promised delivery dates of fixtures and supplies, which often must be ordered from the manufacturer—a process that can take months. Stock up on nails, screws, solder, paint and tools, including special tools such as a basin wrench *(page 88)* or a pipe cutter *(page 105)*, which may have to be borrowed or hired. And don't forget replacement parts—the hacksaw blade always seems to break at a weekend after the hardware shops close.

When you are ready to begin, save time and effort by working in an area as uncluttered as possible. Remove furniture, appliances, fixtures, cabinets and carpeting wherever practical. Working around them, or removing them piecemeal, not only slows things down but exposes them to unnecessary damage. Place doormats at all entrances and hang sheets in open passageways to keep dust and debris out of the rest of the house; if you will be chipping dusty plaster, it is a good idea to wet the sheets first for additional protection.

Allot enough time to do the job thoroughly and without haste, and allow for delays. If you plan to use a professional to handle certain tricky parts of the job, be sure that your schedules are co-ordinated. Your own schedule, though, should be sufficiently flexible to keep you going; do not place yourself in a position where everything comes to a standstill while you wait for a workman who arrives late or not at all.

The best way to minimize the temporary loss of a kitchen or bathroom during remodelling is to work midday or at night, between the peak-use periods of early morning and late afternoon. You may want to set up a temporary kitchen elsewhere in the house, and if you are doing extensive bathroom work in a home with children it might be wise to establish protocol for use of a neighbour's facilities.

Even if you live in countries such as Australia and New Zealand where you are required by law to use a professional plumber, planning and preparation will save both time and money.

Clearing the Way for a Major Renovation

Removing old kitchen and bathroom fixtures to make room for new ones is mainly a task of loosening nuts and bolts. Most sinks, basins, W.C.s and baths can be disconnected with simple tools such as screwdrivers and wrenches, including a basin wrench *(below)*, used in cramped spaces.

Always begin by cutting off the water supply nearest the fixtures. Usually this involves closing the valves on the fixtures' supply lines, but for old fixtures that have no valves, you may have to shut down the entire house supply.

Examine old fixtures carefully to see how they are mounted and connected. You may have to use some of the techniques illustrated here and overleaf to remove them. Old sinks and basins may hang from a wall, rest on a pedestal or be set into a countertop. Tap assemblies may extend down through holes in the fixture or they may not be attached to it at all, extending through holes in the wall or countertop. By comparison, removing a W.C. *(page 90)* is usually easy—though sometimes messy. It takes only a few minutes to empty the cistern and disconnect a W.C. But because a W.C.'s trap is an integral part of the pan, water will remain in it until the pan is tilted, sometimes inadvertently, allowing the water to discharge.

When disconnecting a bath, the side panel hiding the supply and waste pipework must be removed. Usually this involves either prising the side panel away from the timber framework supporting the bath, or undoing the caps and mirror screws securing an access panel.

Once the pipework is disconnected, dismantle the timber framework so that the bath can be removed. This may require careful handling and some brawny helpers. In a small bathroom the W.C. and basin may have to be taken out—even if you must later reinstall them—to provide enough space to manoeuvre the bath from its recess. Steel and plastic baths can be lifted and carried out by two people. But a standard cast-iron bath weighs about 150 kilograms and requires four people to lift it. Unless you plan to re-use the bath, it is often easier to break it up in the bathroom.

In most cases, however, it is possible to salvage all or part of a removed fixture for use elsewhere. But keep in mind that fixtures are fragile and easily damaged when dropped or bumped; china W.C.s can crack, ceramic and vitreous enamel basins are likely to chip and steel sinks can be dented.

You can save parts of a fixture by removing them and making a sketch of the parts before placing them in a container. But remember that the handsome taps from an old basin may not fit a new one.

When fixtures have been removed, it is advisable to seal the open supply lines with caps or plugs of the same material, particularly if there is no valve on the supply line or if water is dripping from the open end *(page 91)*. Severed soil and waste pipework should be temporarily sealed with a plastic bag fastened with masking tape or string, to prevent sewer gas from the drains entering the house. This will also protect the pipes from being clogged by construction debris until they are connected to the new fixtures. If a wall containing pipework is to be broken through or torn down *(pages 92–93)*, the pipes within the wall must be removed, rerouted or cut back to the floor before the openings are sealed.

Removing Sinks and Basins

1 **Disconnecting water supply lines.** Turn off the water supply and open both taps. When the water flow ceases, unscrew the coupling nuts to free the supply pipes from the tap tails; use a basin wrench *(right)* if space is cramped. If there are shut-off valves on the supply lines, also unscrew the coupling nuts above the valves to free the supply lines. If there are no valves, remove the uncoupled supply lines after the sink or basin has been lifted off.

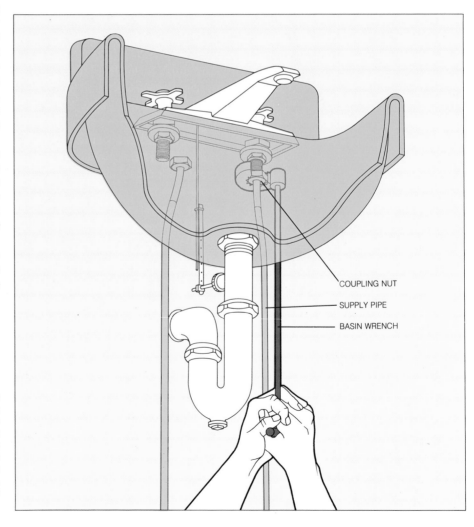

COUPLING NUT

SUPPLY PIPE

BASIN WRENCH

2 **Disconnecting the trap.** Place a bucket beneath the trap and unscrew the cleanout plug to drain it, then unscrew the hexagon nut to free the trap from the tailpiece *(right)* or waste disposal unit. If there is a dishwasher, disconnect its drain hose by loosening the hose clamp *(page 123)*. If you are working on an inset basin with a pop-up waste and a tap assembly fastened to a countertop, disconnect the pop-up retaining nut before removing the basin.

POP-UP
RETAINER NUT

TRAP

3 **Dismounting an inset installation.** Using an old screwdriver, loosen the mastic round the edge of a ceramic basin, then push up from underneath to break the seal; lift the basin away from the countertop *(below)*. Before lifting out a light plastic or vitreous enamel basin, loosen the toothed clamps that hold the rim down on to the countertop surface; working on the underside of the countertop, undo the screws securing each clamp *(inset)* and swing the clamps to one side so that they are clear of the rim.

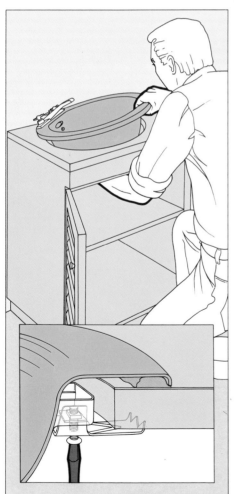

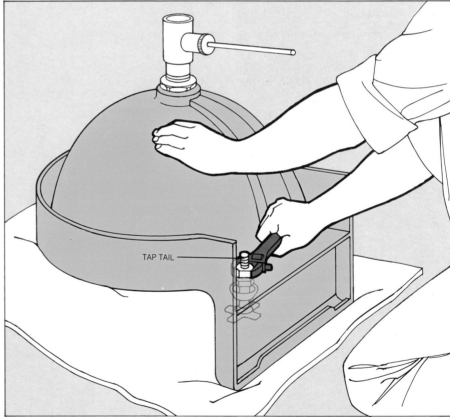

TAP TAIL

4 **Removing taps.** Place the basin face down on the floor—using padding if you intend to re-use it. Unscrew the nuts from the tap tails and lift out the washers. Turn the basin face up and gently knock the taps to break their seal of plumber's putty, then lift out the tap assembly.

Taking Out a W.C.

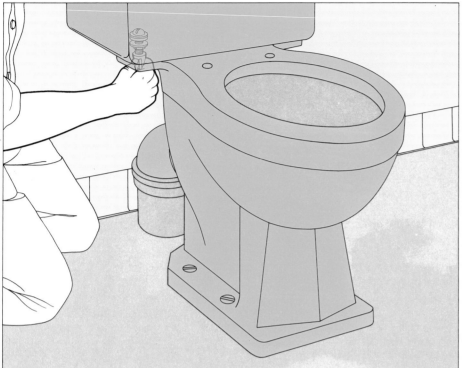

SOIL PIPE

Disconnecting cistern and pan. Turn off the supply valve, flush the W.C., then bail and sponge the remaining water from the cistern and pan. Disconnect the supply line as for a sink line *(page 88)*. If the cistern is mounted on the pan, undo the wing nuts under the pan's rear rim *(above)*, using a helper if necessary to hold a screwdriver on the boltheads, to keep them from turning. If the cistern is wall-mounted, remove the L-shaped flush pipe connecting it to the pan by

loosening the hexagon nut at the cistern end and easing it out of the rubber seal that attaches it to the pan. Then remove the screws or bolts that hold the cistern to the wall. Undo the screws that secure the pan to the floor. If the pan is attached to the soil pipe by a push-fit rubber connector, ease the pan outlet from the connector; if there is a putty or mastic seal, rock the bowl to break the seal, then lift it free.

Clearing a cement joint. Where a pan has been cemented to a cast-iron or stoneware soil pipe, use a heavy hammer to break the pan outlet in front of the joint. Stuff a rag into the soil outlet to prevent debris falling in, then carefully chisel out the pan fragments and cement *(above)*. Where the pan itself has been cemented to the floor, break the seal with a cold chisel. If re-using the pan, carefully chip away the cement joint until you can ease the pan out.

Taking Out a Bath

1 **Disconnecting the waste and overflow.** Loosen the hexagon nut connecting the trap to the waste and overflow pipe *(right)*. If the overflow pipe is connected to the trap itself, release it from the bath by unscrewing its outlet inside the bath. Do this by hand or insert two screwdrivers into two of the outlet cap's holes; then, grasping the screwdrivers in one hand, use a bar placed between them to turn them in an anti-clockwise direction *(inset)*.

Sometimes an overflow pipe discharges directly through an outside wall. After freeing the bath, saw the overflow pipe flush with the wall and fill the hole with a proprietary filler. If a new bath is to be installed in the same position, fit it with a combined waste and overflow pipe—outside overflow pipes can cause cold draughts and may even lead to frozen pipes.

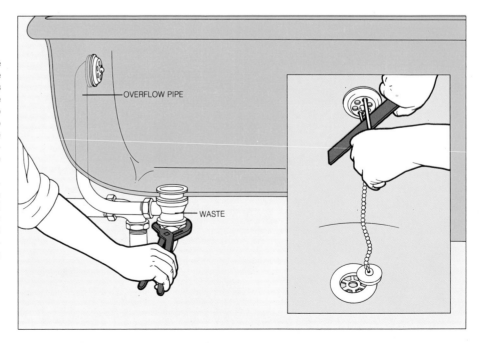

OVERFLOW PIPE

WASTE

2 **Freeing the bath rim.** If there is a tiled wall round the bath, use a cold chisel and hammer to chip away the first course of tiles above the bath *(right)* to free the rim. Wear goggles to protect your eyes from flying fragments of tile. If the bath is acrylic or plastic, it will have wall mounting brackets supporting its rim: unscrew these brackets from the wall.

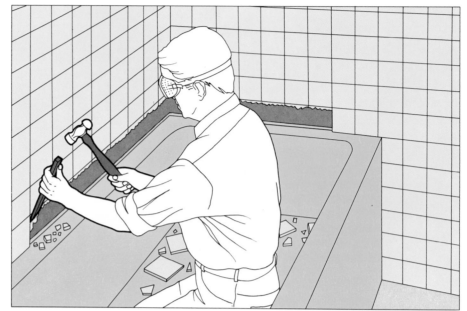

3 **Removing the bath.** To lower the level of the bath, use a wrench to move the bolts holding the cradle brackets or feet of the bath. Grip the nut at the base of each threaded bolt and turn clockwise *(right)*. Prise the bath away from the wall and have someone help you carry it away.

If you are taking out a cast-iron bath that you are not re-using, you may wish to demolish it on site rather than try and remove it. Wrap the bath in a thick covering such as an old blanket and shatter it with a sledge hammer or club hammer. Wear goggles and protective clothing.

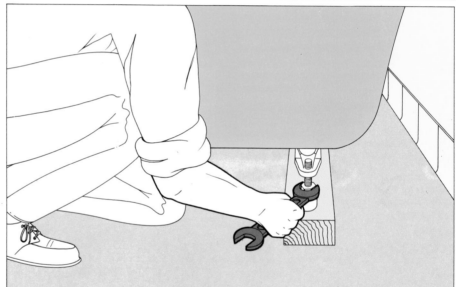

Capping Pipes

Whenever there will be any delay between the removal of a fixture and the installation of a new one, or if a valve allows water to drip from an open end, pipes should be tightly capped. If the pipe is threaded, screw on a cap of the same material. Elbows and short pipe extenders, which have female threads, require plugs. For unthreaded copper pipes, solder on a capillary cap or fit a brass compression cap. Specially adapted compression caps are available to fit on many plastic materials such as polythene and cPVC.

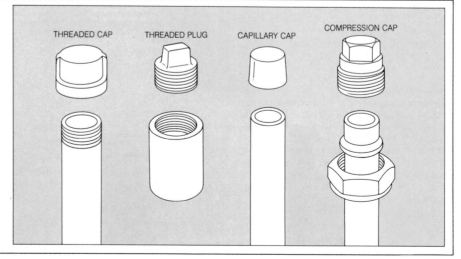

THREADED CAP   THREADED PLUG   CAPILLARY CAP   COMPRESSION CAP

Tearing Down an Old Wall

To create space for a new bathroom or an expanded kitchen you may be able to remove all or part of an interior wall. Walls that are non-loadbearing can be quickly torn down without weakening the structure of your house. Avoid tearing down a load-bearing wall which requires support such as a rolled steel joist. Walls running the same way as the ceiling joists and which do not support another wall above are non-loadbearing. Before removing any wall or part of one, check that you can re-route or cut back pipes and cables passing through the wall.

To remove a stud wall, begin by skinning the wall. Power tools often used to remove the surfaces of the wall cannot be used on tiled walls. Instead, the tiles and materials under it are broken up with a heavy hammer and ripped free (Step 1). To save the tiles, though, prise them off before attacking the wall (page 8). If your wall is plasterboard, plaster or panelling, the job can be done faster by using a circular saw, set to the depth of the wall covering, to saw out sections between the studs (page 56, Step 1). Demolishing the skeleton of a stud wall and patching the gaps is done the same way, whatever the skinning method.

Knocking down a solid wall involves the same techniques whether the wall is constructed of blocks or bricks (opposite page, below). With some constructions, a non-loadbearing wall may continue through the ceiling as far as the underside of the floor above. If this is the case, remove this section of the wall carefully as you work along the top course. Double check first, however, that the wall does not continue through the floor and the room above, as this would mean it was a load-bearing wall.

To minimize the spread of dust, hang dustsheets either side of the wall being knocked down. Always wear goggles when removing a wall; use a dust mask, as well, with a lath and plaster wall. Don protective gloves when tearing away at a wall surface, particularly a tile one. Strong leather shoes protect feet from falling masonry.

Removing a Stud Wall

1 Tearing away the wall surface. Turn off the power to any circuits running to or through the wall to be demolished. Smash up the plasterboard between the studs on one side of the wall, using a heavy hammer. Wear protective gloves to rip the broken sections free. Use a crowbar to lever the stubborn bits of plasterboard from the studs to which they are nailed. In a lath and plaster wall, use your hammer to break up the plaster and lath, finally prising any remaining strips of wood lath from the studs with the crowbar.

2 Removing the second wall surface. In the same room, hammer free the back of the plasterboard panels—or the strips of wood lath supporting a plaster wall—along the length of the studs to which they are nailed. Then use your hands to push entire plasterboard panels free of the studs and into the adjoining room. With plaster walls, chunks will fall into the next room and you can then rip or prise the laths free from the studs. Cut all but the end studs in half and work the halves free from the head and sole plate.

3 **Removing the end studs and head and sole plate.** Make two saw cuts about 50 mm apart midway down the end stud or sole plate. Chisel out the wood between the cuts and prise up one half of the member. Hold a block of wood in the gap left by the half just removed and use it as a fulcrum to lever up the second half *(left)*. Prise the head away from the ceiling and the sole plate from the floor and repair any damage caused by the removed nails. If the head was set into the ceiling and has left a gap, fill this with plaster-board strips nailed to the ceiling joists, place scrim cloth over the joints and skim with plaster.

Knocking Down a Solid Wall

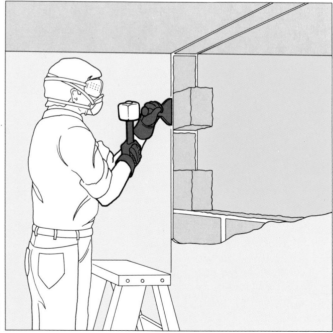

1 **Opening up the wall.** First make sure the wall is non-loadbearing. Use a bolster and lump hammer to chisel away a 600 by 600 mm area of wall surface from the top centre of the wall. Then knock out one or two blocks from the top course or, in the case of a brick wall, the top two or three courses.

2 **Knocking down the wall.** Working along each course, knock the blocks off one by one by hitting them near the vertical mortar joint with the lump hammer; steady each piece with your free hand. You should be able to judge where the mortar joints are without removing any more of the wall surface. Trim the protruding blocks at the end of alternate rows by placing the bolster on the side of the block, in line with the opening, and giving it a sharp blow with the hammer.

How to Run Pipes Through and Along Walls and Floors

Building or rebuilding a kitchen or bathroom may mean constructing walls—not just partitions, but a special kind called wet walls. A wet wall provides space for pipework—particularly for the larger waste and soil pipes—and is therefore thicker than an ordinary partition.

The easiest way to provide a new wet wall, if your plan and space permit, is to add one to an existing wall. Run the pipes along the surface of the old wall and attach them to it. Then nail battens to the wall *(below)* and cover the pipes with a new wall surface. This gives a neat finish but reduces a room's dimensions. Alternatively, box in pipes; fix battens alongside them and cover them with plywood or hardboard *(opposite, above)*. This solution is ideal for countries such as Australia and New Zealand where pipes must be accessible.

When such short cuts are not possible you must then erect a new wet wall *(pages 96–98)*. It is generally 150 mm thick, instead of the normal 100 mm, and 150 by 50 mm timbers are used for the horizontal head and sole plates. They may also be used for the vertical studs, but the simpler construction shown here uses 100 by 50 mm studs set sideways and staggered so that there is space to thread pipes between studs, eliminating the need to drill holes.

The way the wet wall is installed depends on the direction of the floor and ceiling joists. If the new wall will run at right angles to the joists, nail or screw the head and sole plates to the edge of each floor and ceiling joist that they cross. If the new wall will run parallel to the joists, position the frame under the most convenient ceiling joist, and nail or screw the head plate to that joist through the ceiling. If you must locate the wall between joists, remove sections of the ceiling and install nailing blocks *(page 96, above, right)*.

Since a new wet wall is non-loadbearing, the placement of the studs is not crucial. Usually set 600 mm apart, if the position of one interferes with the placement of a fixture, reposition it.

Supply pipes can be run through 100 mm-thick stud partition walls by cutting holes or notches in their framing, but it is not wise to install the larger soil and waste pipes as the cuts will weaken the framework. Pipes can be run under suspended timber floors, but avoid running them through joists which form part of the basic house structure. If you must run pipes through joists, never cut notches deeper than one-fifth of the joist's depth, and if possible position them near joist ends.

Another method of disguising pipes, but one only suitable for narrow bore supply pipes, is to sink them into a solid wall *(opposite, below)*. Keep a record of where you have sunk pipes, for future reference.

An Easy Way to Make a Wet Wall

Battening the wall. After connecting your pipework *(pages 102–112)*, bracket the pipes to the wall. Some types of bracket have a single fixing screw; these either have to be installed before connecting the pipe, or the pipe has to be eased to one side to allow the clips to be fixed along its centre line. Then, cut strips of wood thick enough to project just beyond the pipes and screw these vertically to the wall at intervals along the entire length of the wall. Before nailing new plasterboard panels to the battens, make holes in the panels where the new pipework will connect through to the fixtures. Leave an access panel in the plasterboard over the new connections where push-fit or compression fittings have been used.

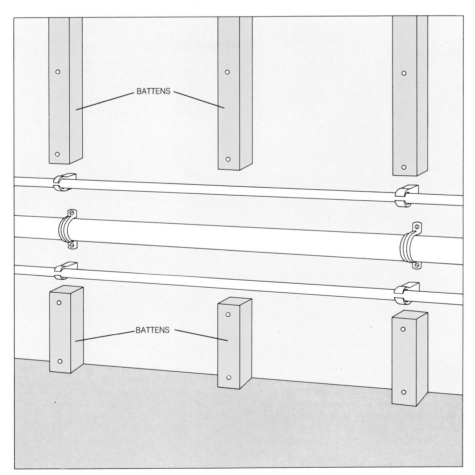

BATTENS

BATTENS

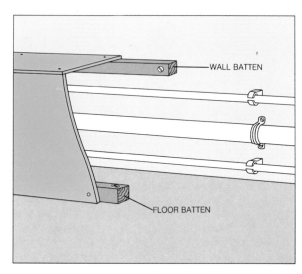

WALL BATTEN

FLOOR BATTEN

Boxing in Pipes

Constructing the box. Fix a 25 by 25 mm batten to the wall just above the pipework and another one to the floor a few millimetres in front of the pipework, using 40 mm No. 8 countersunk wood screws. Measure from the floor to the top of the wall batten and cut a length of 15 or 20 mm plywood to size. Pin the plywood to the floor batten using 40 mm lost-head nails and, with a spirit level, check that it is vertical. Measure from the wall to the front face of the panel you have just fixed and cut a second length of plywood to this width. Fix it to the wall batten and to the edge of the front panel with lost-head nails.

Hiding Pipes in Solid Walls

1 Cutting a chase. Draw parallel chase lines about 100 mm apart on the wall where you intend to run the pipe. Working along the chase lines with a lump hammer and bolster, chop through the thickness of the plaster to reveal the wall. Check that the pipe fits into the chase once it has been wrapped *(below, left)*; if it does not, chisel deeper into the wall. For a 15 mm pipe, you will need a 20 mm-deep chase.

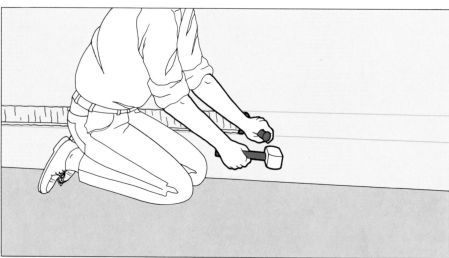

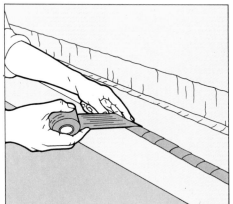

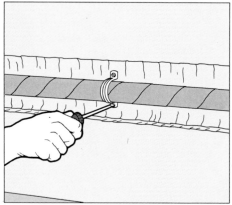

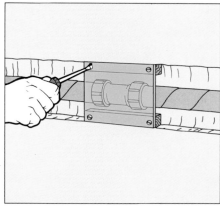

2 Wrapping the pipe. Wrap grease-impregnated tape round the copper pipe to protect it from corrosion and to accommodate expansion. Connect the pipe and then turn on the water supply to test the connections before wrapping the soldered joints.

3 Fixing the saddles. Secure the pipe to the wall with copper saddles. To fix a saddle, place it over the pipe and, with a pencil, mark the screw hole positions on the wall. Remove the saddle, drill and plug the holes. Replace the saddle and screw it to the wall using two 25 mm No. 7 brass screws. Repeat at regular intervals *(page 100)*.

4 Making an access panel. Use plugs and screws to fix battens into the chase on either side of a compression joint or valve. Cut a plywood or hardboard cover to fit over the joint flush with the finish plaster. Screw the access panel into position and plaster over all recessed pipework up to the edge of the panel. If you are using cPVC pipe, place a layer of paper or card over the pipe before plastering to allow for expansion.

A New Wall Designed for Piping

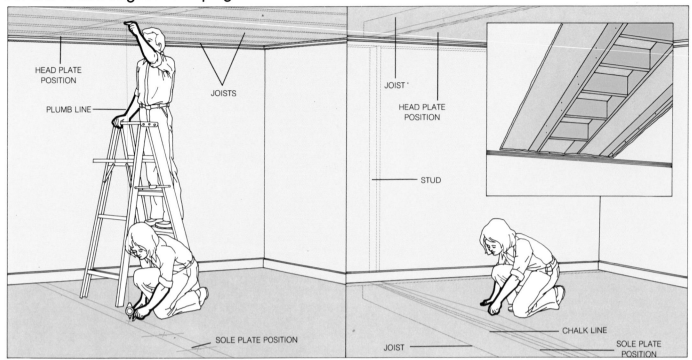

HEAD PLATE POSITION

PLUMB LINE

JOISTS

SOLE PLATE POSITION

JOIST

HEAD PLATE POSITION

STUD

JOIST

CHALK LINE

SOLE PLATE POSITION

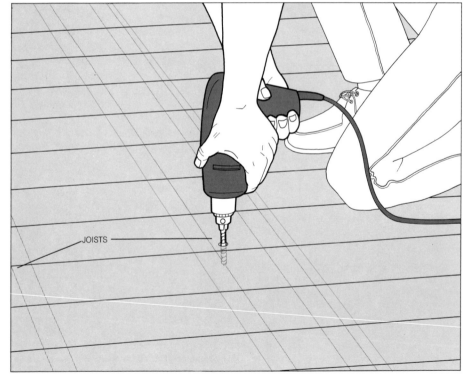

JOISTS

1 **Locating the head and sole plate.** For new walls that run at right angles to the room joists, simply mark the position of the head on the ceiling and use a plumb line to find the corresponding spot on the floor for the sole plate *(above, left)*. If the new wall runs parallel to the room joists, find the ceiling joist nearest to the intended spot for the frame and position the sole plate and head so that the edge of the new wall frame overlaps the joist. Mark both positions with a chalk line *(above, right)*.

If you must locate the wall between joists, cut away the ceiling to expose the two closest joists, then install a series of nailing blocks, of the same size timber as the joists, at 600 mm intervals between the joists *(inset)*. After installing the blocks, patch the strip with plasterboard.

2 **Cutting holes for the supply.** Drill a small locating hole within the chalk lines; drill 50 mm to one side of the floorboard nails to be certain of clearing the joist. Check that the edge of the joist is clear of the hole by at least half the diameter of the pipe. Use a brace and bit or a hole saw to enlarge the hole to a few milli- metres wider than the diameter of the pipe. If the pipe is to pass through a ceiling below, remove the section of floorboard through which you have just drilled and use a hole saw to cut a corresponding hole in the ceiling. Where you need to run more than one pipe, always try to group them together.

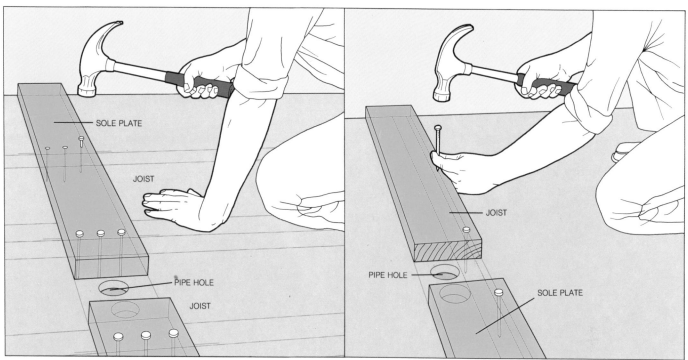

SOLE PLATE

JOIST

PIPE HOLE

JOIST

JOIST

PIPE HOLE

SOLE PLATE

3 **Installing the sole plate.** Remove the skirting board from the two walls the new wet wall will touch. Cut two pieces of 150 by 50 mm timber the length of the distance between the two walls. Use one length as the sole plate and lay it in place on the floor. Mark the position of the holes for the supply pipes and cut the sole plate across its width about 25 mm to each side of the holes. Reposition the two parts of the sole plate and nail them to the floor joists with 100 mm wire or lost-head nails; drive in three nails at each joist *(above, left)*. If the sole plate runs parallel to floor joists, nail the sole plate at 300 mm intervals, 20 mm from the edge of the plate *(above, right)*.

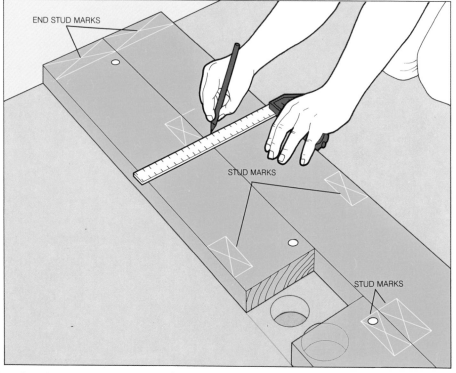

END STUD MARKS

STUD MARKS

STUD MARKS

4 **Marking the head and sole plate.** Mark positions for end studs at the ends of the sole plate. Then along one edge of the sole plate, mark positions at 600 mm intervals for one row of intervening studs. Along the other edge of the sole plate, mark positions for a second row of studs, each set midway between a pair in the first row. Place the head beside the sole plate and, with a combination square, transfer the stud marks from the sole plate to the head *(above)*.

5 **Assembling the frame.** To determine the length of the studs, drop a plumb line from the ceiling to the floor at three points, and measure the height of the plumb line at each point; the three measurements should be within a few millimetres of one another. Take the minimum measurement (to make sure the frame will fit under the ceiling), subtract 100 mm for the combined thicknesses of the head and sole plates and cut to this length two 150 by 50 mm end studs and the necessary number of 100 by 50 mm studs. Nail the end studs in place through the head plate. Lay intermediate studs on the floor, butt their ends to the head plate and nail them in place; turn the frame over and repeat for the second row of studs.

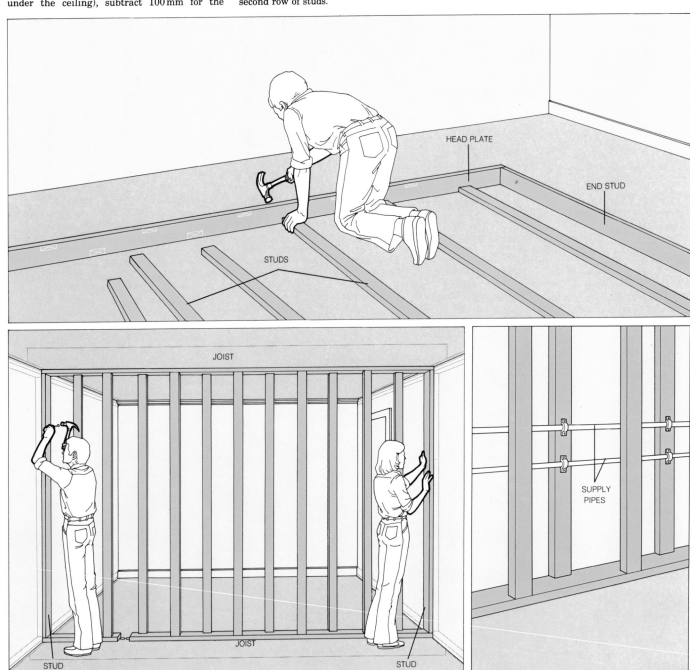

HEAD PLATE

END STUD

STUDS

JOIST

STUD

STUD

JOIST

SUPPLY PIPES

6 **Installing the wet-wall frame.** With a helper, lift the frame and place it on the sole plate so that the end studs rest on the sole-plate marks. Nail the head to a ceiling joist or joists, using the method on page 97, above. Nail the end studs to studs in the abutting walls. If the frame runs at right angles to the joists, only nail the end studs to the walls if you are certain that a stud stands directly behind each end stud. For solid walls drill and plug them and screw the studs to the wall. Toenail the end studs to the sole plate. Position each 100 by 50 mm stud on the sole plate, check it is vertical with a level, shim it if necessary, then toenail it in place.

7 **Supporting the pipes.** Run the new pipes between the back and front studs, clamping the pipe to either row of studs. Use brackets designed for the type of pipe you are using (page 100) and secure the pipe to each stud along its path.

A Partition and a Door Set

An ordinary partition wall resembles the wet wall described on pages 94–98—with two important differences. The head and sole plates of a partition wall are 100 by 50 mm rather than 150 by 50 mm, and the studs are set across the sole plate rather than parallel to it. Like a wet wall, the partition is finished with plasterboard.

Installing a door in this type of wall is a simple matter of nailing or screwing the frame of a factory-made door set to the sides and top of a doorway—technically, a rough doorframe—built into the partition. The doorway consists of two outer studs to which are nailed two jack studs; a horizontal crosspiece, called a header, tops the jack studs, and a short vertical stud, called a cripple stud, stands between the header and the head plate.

The door set comprises a frame mounted with doorstop, keep plate and hinges; a door fitted with a mortise latch; and pre-cut and mitred architrave. The frame comes in three ready-jointed sections, a head and two jambs, which are easily assembled on site.

Doors are generally 1981 or 2044 mm high, and 526 to 826 mm wide. Buy the door set before you build the partition frame, and use the door set's measurements as starting points for the built-in doorway. Cover the completed frame with plasterboard to the edges of the doorway, then install the door assembly itself.

Door sets are sold by most builders' merchants, but if they are not available in your area, the frame, door and architrave can be purchased separately.

Building the wall and doorway. Nail a 100 by 50 mm sole plate to the floor for the new wall and build a wall frame using 100 by 50 mm studs and head plate. Follow the method shown on pages 97–98, but set the studs across the plates, and space them 600 mm apart to save timber. Omit the studs that would stand in the doorway.

For the rough doorframe, install two ordinary studs as the outer studs, and space them 100 mm farther apart than the width of the head of the door assembly. Cut two jack studs 32 mm shorter than the top of the head and nail them to the outer studs, flush with the bottoms of the studs. Nail a 100 by 50 mm header between the outer studs and across the tops of the jack studs, and nail a 100 by 50 mm cripple stud between the header and the head plate. Install the wall frame on the sole plate *(opposite page, Step 6)* and complete the doorframe by cutting away the part of the sole plate lying between the jack studs.

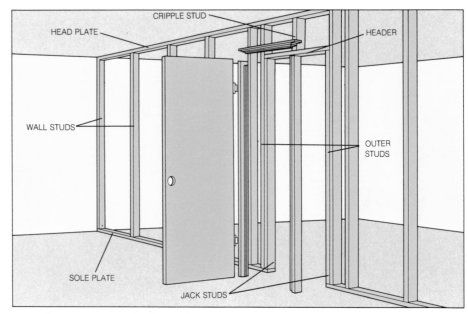

Installing a Door Set

1 Fixing the doorframe. Assemble the head and two jambs following the manufacturer's instructions. Place the frame in the rough doorway so that any protrusions on either side of the wall are equal and check with a spirit level that the frame is level and plumb. Push shims between the jack studs and the doorframe; check again that the frame is level and plumb and nail the frame to the jack studs *(above)*.

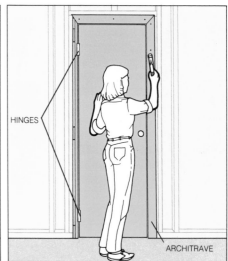

2 Finishing the job. Hang the door and finish the door opening by nailing the architrave round the door *(above)* with 37 mm lost-head or oval nails staggered at 150 to 250 mm intervals, and allowing a 6 mm margin between the inside of the architrave and the doorframe. Nail the head first so that you can check that the jambs will fit; plane them if necessary.

Supporting Pipes and Fixtures

All bathroom fixtures require special supports, adapted to the type and location of the fixture. Many sinks and basins are supported by kitchen worktops or vanity units, but some basin models are bracketed to the wall on their underside. If a basin is to be mounted on partition or wet wall, a crosspiece will have to be installed in order to provide support *(right, top)*. A pedestal or vanity basin has the advantage over a wall-mounted model in providing a means of concealing the pipework, as well as providing additional support.

Baths, the largest fixtures, also need support. Acrylic and plastic models rest in a cradle to prevent the bath from sagging when it is full of water *(opposite page)*. In addition, all baths, particularly the heavy steel and the even heavier cast-iron baths, should have pieces of hardwood or plywood secured under their brackets or feet to distribute the weight over the floor.

Some shower trays are supplied with a cradle to raise them above floor level, allowing for the easy installation of waste pipe and trap. Where no cradle is provided, you can construct a wooden plinth to raise the tray and to allow subsequent access to the trap *(opposite page, below)*.

Pipework also must be supported. There is a wide range of brackets available enabling any pipe size or material to be fixed to any type of surface. Soil, waste and some supply pipes are supported by brackets screwed to the wall after the pipework has been assembled. Some of the brackets for supply pipes, however, must be fixed to the wall before the pipework is positioned. If this is the case, the pipe route is pencilled on to the wall and the brackets are then fixed along the line. Double brackets allow supply pipes to be run side by side with only one fixing. Wherever possible, plastic clips should be used in preference to metal ones as they resist the transfer of heat into the wall and reduce the risk of frozen pipes.

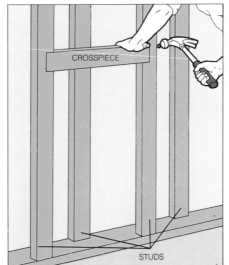

CROSSPIECE

STUDS

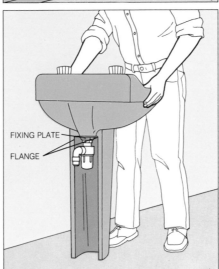

FIXING PLATE

FLANGE

Supports for Basins

A crosspiece for a wet wall. Cut a 100 by 50 mm crosspiece 40 mm longer than the distance between studs. Hold the piece across the two studs at the basin position, with each end of the crosspiece overlapping a stud by 20 mm; check the horizontal alignment of the piece with a level, then mark the top and bottom of the piece on the studs. With a hammer and chisel, notch the studs within the marks, wedge the crosspiece into the notches with the front of the piece flush to the fronts of the studs, and nail the piece securely in place. Cover the wall with plasterboard and screw the basin bracket to the crosspiece through the wall surface.

A pedestal for a basin. Assemble the waste fitting *(page 117)*, slipping on the pedestal's fixing plate before tightening the back nut, and attach the trap to the waste. Lower the basin on to the pedestal *(left)* and secure the two by tightening the retaining screws through the holes in the fixing plate into the flange. Then position the basin and pedestal, check that the basin is level and mark the screw holes on to the wall and, if there are any in the pedestal, on the floor. Pencil in the outline of the back of the basin and the pedestal base, so that you can reposition them exactly after preparing the screw holes.

Supporting Pipes

Size of Pipe (mm)	Horizontal Spacing (mm)	Vertical Spacing (mm)
uPVC		
32, 40	500	1200
50	600	1200
75, 100	900	1800
cPVC		
15, 28	500	100
Copper		
8, 10	1200	1800
15, 28	1800	2400

Correct spacing for brackets. All pipework must be adequately supported in order to prevent it from sagging and to stop vibration. The maximum distances recommended between brackets along the pipe for various pipe materials and sizes are set out in the chart above. The first bracket is usually placed approximately 300 mm from the starting point of the run. Brackets should also be installed within 300 mm of any change of direction in the pipe.

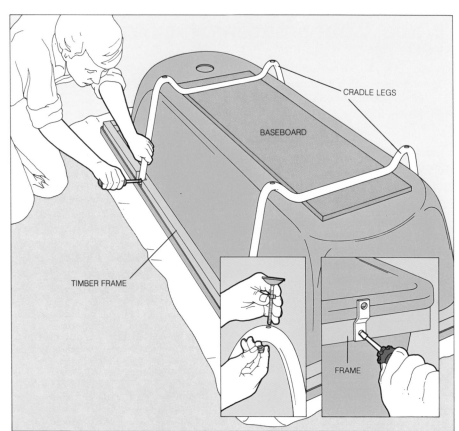

A Cradle for a Plastic Bath

1 **Assembling the cradle.** Place the bath upside down on an old blanket. Slip the two cradle legs over the bath and screw them to the timber rim frame *(left)* and then to the baseboard. Use only the screws provided by the manufacturer for the baseboard, otherwise you risk making a hole in the bath. Slot the four leg bolts into the holes in the cradle feet, securing them into position with a nut on either side of the foot *(left inset)*. Turn the bath over and screw the wall-mounting brackets to the timber frame *(right inset)*.

A Support for a Shower Tray

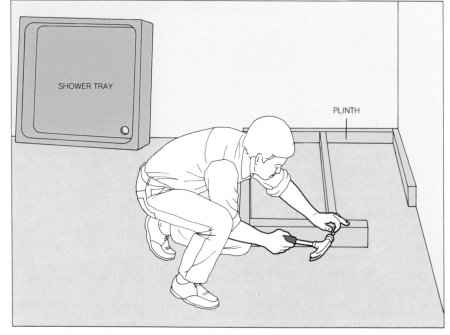

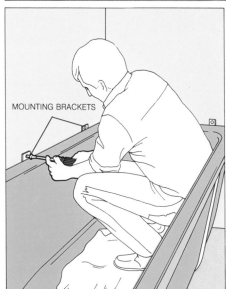

2 **Adjusting the bath height.** Put two 100 by 25 mm lengths of hardwood or plywood on the floor where the cradle legs will stand; with a helper, lift the bath in its frame and place it in position. Move the lower nut on the leg bolts up or down to adjust the bath height and check for level. Screw the feet cups to the wood. Finally, attach the mounting brackets to the wall *(above)*.

Making a plinth. Nail or screw together five lengths of 50 mm timber *(above)*. Cut away a section or corner and make a removable panel to allow access to the trap and waste. You may also have to cut a hole in the plinth for the waste pipe exit. Nail or screw the plinth to the floor. The height of the plinth should be equal to the distance between the base of the shower tray and the bottom of the fitted waste trap, plus 30 mm. If you wish to face the plinth with tiles or other material, make its perimeter slightly less than that of the shower tray.

Getting Rid of Soil and Waste: Connecting into the Stack

A trouble-free drainage installation takes careful planning and execution. In a limited space, you must accommodate pipes for all new fixtures, slope them downwards towards a large vertical pipe called a stack, and possibly, depending on the distance of new fixtures from the existing stack, run new vent pipes *(pages 106–107)*.

Most modern homes will probably have a single PVC stack, running down the inside of an exterior wall, that receives soil from the W.C.s and waste water from other fixtures. Older houses will have two stacks, both outside the house; the waste stack, which receives only waste water, and the soil stack, into which the W.C.s discharge.

In the U.K., adding to your waste system above ground does not require local authority permission, but in Australia and New Zealand this work can only be done by a licensed plumber. If you are in any doubt about your plans, consult the authority before starting work—you could be liable to a fine if you contravene the water by-laws or building regulations.

The job has been made easier for amateur plumbers by PVC pipes and fittings, which can be fitted into systems where other materials have been used. PVC pipe is lightweight, durable and easily joined with solvent cement or push-fit connections which incorporate a rubber sealing ring. It can be cut with a saw, but you must make straight cuts at right angles to the pipe; to be sure of your cuts, you may prefer a tenon saw and mitre box or a pipe cutter with a special wheel for cutting plastics.

Because pipes and fittings must carry the flow of wastes by gravity alone, the interior of a completed installation should offer a smooth continuous surface and as few sharp turns as possible. A waste or soil pipe must slope downwards at a ratio dictated by the pipe's diameter and length, as well as by the type of fixture *(chart, right)*; too shallow a fall will encourage clogging, and one too steep could cause the water seal in a trap to be siphoned out.

All soil and waste runs begin with a trap—a U-shaped section of pipe in which water collects to block the passage of sewer gases. Toilets have built-in traps; all other fixtures have a separate assembly.

Two types of trap in common use are the P-trap and the S-trap: the P-trap has a near-horizontal exit from the U; the S-trap's exit is vertically downwards. P-traps are preferable because the exit line allows you to comply with the recommended falls *(chart, below)*. Also the water seal is less likely to be siphoned out.

Beyond the trap, fixtures other than a W.C. may discharge separately and directly into the stack via a tee joint or boss connector. A fixture may also be connected by a swept tee to a sloping waste pipe, which in turn branches into the stack. To connect a W.C. outlet to the existing stack, a section of the stack must be cut out and a tee fitting inserted *(pages 104–105)*.

When branching in a W.C. with other new fixtures, use a special branch fitting which has sockets on both sides of the W.C. inlet, allowing waste pipes to be boss connected. If you are adding a waste to a stack in the vicinity of an existing W.C. branch, use a boss connector and fit this either above the tee or at least 203 mm below the centre line of its branch.

When installing your new waste and soil routes, use the recommended pipe diameters: in the U.K. 100 mm for W.C. branches and main soil or combined soil and waste stacks; 65 or 75 mm for vertical branch waste stacks; 50 mm for a combined bath and basin waste; 40 mm for baths, sinks, washing machines and dishwashers, and 32 mm for wash basins and bidets. Use fittings incorporating cleaning eyes wherever blockages are likely to occur.

The Correct Slope for Every Waste Pipe

Fixture	Maximum fall	Distance from trap to main stack without venting (mm)
W.C.	1:20	up to 6000
Basin	1:12	0–750
Bidet	1:20	750–1000
Bath	1:30	1000–1250
Sink	1:36	1250–1500
Shower	1:48	1500–1700
Bath		
Sink	1:48	1700–2300
Shower		

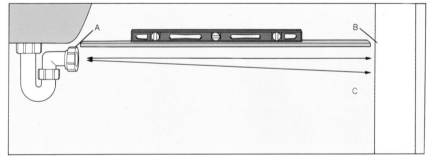

Calculating the fall. Slope a new waste pipe according to the fall recommended for the fixture. For a W.C. the fall is constant whatever the distance between the crown of its trap and the stack, but for other fixtures the fall will vary *(chart, above)*. To calculate the point at which a new waste pipe should enter the stack, hold the fixture, in this case a basin, with the trap attached, against the wall and mark the wall at the height of the trap crown "A" *(above)*. Place a length of wood between "A" and the stack, check it is level and mark the stack at point "B". Measure the distance between "A" and "B"; providing this does not exceed the maximum recommended distance without venting from trap to main stack *(page 106)*, divide by the appropriate fall and the result will give the distance to measure down from point "B" to point "C", the centre for the new branch fitting.

Making a Boss Connection into the Stack

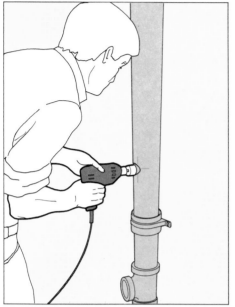

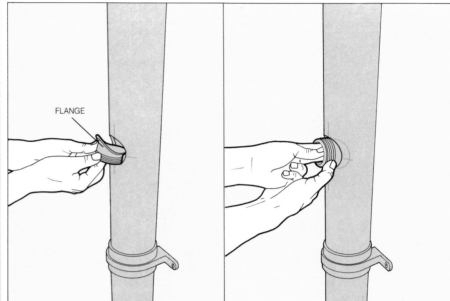

FLANGE

1 **Cutting the hole.** Calculate the fall line from the fixture to the stack *(chart, opposite)* and mark the connection point. Using an electric drill and hole cutter attachment, cut a hole in the stack; check the manufacturer's instructions as to the correct size of cutter.

2 **Inserting the boss.** Slide the boss, flange facing upwards, through the hole. Holding the boss firmly, turn upright, rotate 90 degrees and pull towards you. The flange should rest comfortably in the inner curve of the stack *(above, right)*. Take care not to let go of the boss.

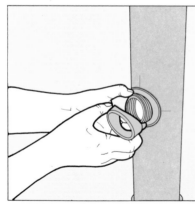

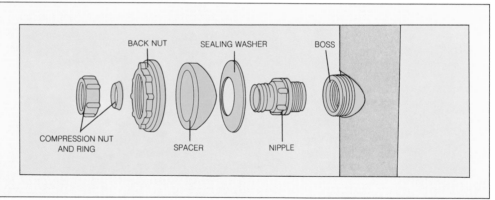

BACK NUT   SEALING WASHER   BOSS

COMPRESSION NUT
AND RING   SPACER   NIPPLE

3 **Securing the boss.** Still taking care not to let the boss fall into the stack, slip the soft sealing washer and rigid spacer over the boss's outer thread and tighten the back nut firmly against the sealing washer. Wrap PTFE tape round the thread of the plastic nipple and screw the nipple into the inner thread of the boss.

COMPRESSION NUT

COMPRESSION RING

4 **Attaching the waste pipe.** Slip the compression nut and ring, with the taper facing the stack, over the waste pipe. Push the pipe as far as it will go into the nipple and tighten the compression nut on to the nipple thread.

Connecting to a PVC Stack

1 Marking for the first cut. Calculate the fall line *(chart, page 102)* and mark the centre point for the connection on to the stack. Hold the tee connector against the stack, aligning the centre of its branch with the mark on the stack and pencil on to the stack the level of the lower socket's tube stop *(below)*.

2 Cutting out the section. Saw through the stack at the mark you have just made. Add 200 mm to the length of the tee and mark the stack this distance up from the first cut. Saw through the pipe at this mark and remove the section of pipe, then chamfer the severed stack ends with a rasp or coarse file *(inset)*.

3 Fitting the tee. Clean the chamfered stack ends and the inside lower socket of the tee. Apply solvent cement to the inside of the socket as far as the tube stop and for the equivalent distance to the lower stack end. Push the tee down on to the stack as far as it will go, twisting it slightly to spread the cement evenly *(below)*. Make sure that the branch connection is facing in the right direction before the cement sets: leave to set, checking the manufacturer's instructions for the correct setting time.

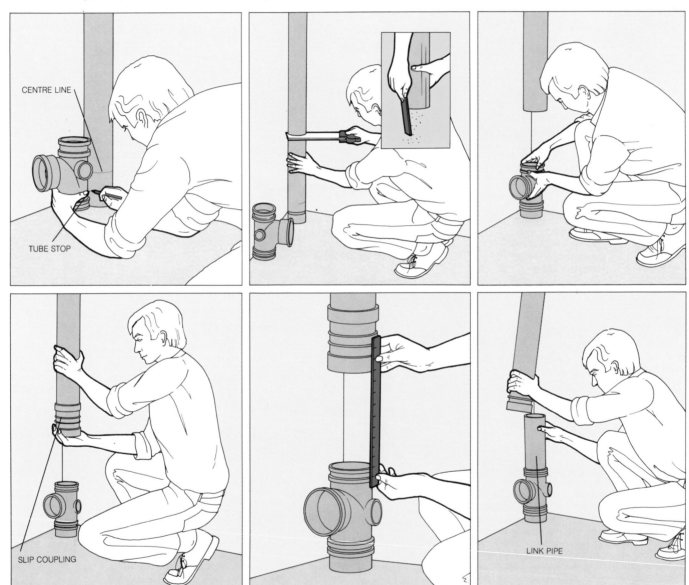

CENTRE LINE

TUBE STOP

SLIP COUPLING

LINK PIPE

4 Inserting the slip coupling. Apply a special lubricant for plastic to the top stack end and to the inside of the slip coupling. Then place the coupling over the stack and push it up until its lower end is level with the stack's end *(above)*.

5 Measuring for the link pipe. Measure the distance between the tube stop of the tee's top socket and the lower rim in the centre rib of the slip coupling *(above)*. Cut a section to this length from the piece of stack removed earlier.

6 Inserting the link pipe. Chamfer both ends of the link pipe then prepare one end and the top socket of the tee for solvent welding *(Step 3, above)*. Ease the top stack end to one side, insert the link pipe in the tee's top socket and push it down, twisting slightly, until it reaches the tube stop.

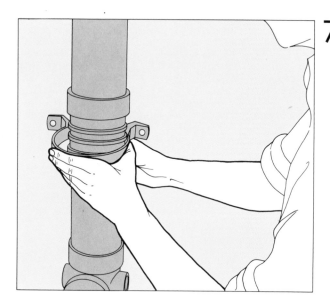

7 **Completing the installation.** Measure from the lower rim of the slip coupling's centre rib to its bottom edge and mark the link pipe this distance below its open end. Apply lubricant to the outside of the link pipe's open end, then slide the slip coupling down over it until its edge meets the pencil mark. Push the wall-fixing bracket into position over the central rib of the coupling *(left)* and screw it to the wall. Then complete the branch and connect the W.C. *(pages 120–121).*

Connecting a W.C. to a Cast-Iron Stack

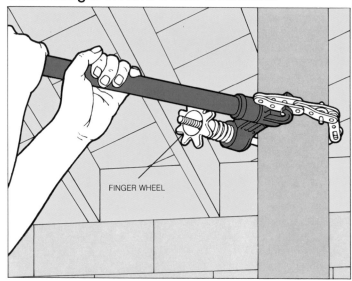

FINGER WHEEL

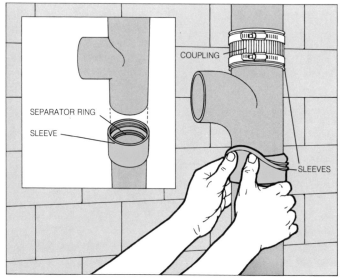

COUPLING

SEPARATOR RING

SLEEVE

SLEEVES

1 **Opening the stack.** Hold a special tee fitting without sockets, chosen to fit the existing stack and the new soil branch, against the stack at the proper height to receive the soil branch *(chart, page 102)* and mark the positions of the top and bottom of the tee on the stack.

To cut the stack use a pipe cutter like the one shown above, which can be hired from most suppliers. Bring the cutting chain around the stack and slip it into the hooks on the other side of the tool head. Set the chain 5 mm above the top mark on the stack, tighten the finger wheel to compress the spring, and move the handle of the cutter back and forth, continuing to tighten the finger wheel, until the pipe separates. Make a second cut 5 mm lower than the bottom mark, remove the section of pipe and stuff toilet paper loosely into the bottom cut end of the stack.

2 **Installing the tee.** Slide the stainless steel ring of a pipe coupling on to the bottom of the cut stack. Fit the neoprene sleeve of the coupling over the pipe with the separator ridge inside the sleeve resting against the end of the pipe *(inset)*. Roll the sleeve on the bottom part of the stack back upon itself until the upper half is folded over the lower half. Repeat the process on the top part of the stack, folding the free end of the sleeve up. Place the tee between the rolled sleeves, fold the sleeves over the ends of the tee, then slide the stainless steel rings over the sleeves and tighten the screws. Use another pipe coupling to connect the soil branch pipe to the tee.

Letting the Drains Breathe

In every soil stack, and combined waste and soil stack, a vertical section rises above the highest fixture in the house. This section is called the stack vent, and is crucial to the drainage system. It releases noxious gases outside the house, and admits air to maintain atmospheric pressure in the pipework. This protects the water seals in the traps around the house from the adverse effects of varying pressures.

A separate waste stack may also have a vertical stack vent, but in older houses it is more common for upstairs bath and basin wastes to discharge into a hopper head fixed to an outside wall which—as it is open to the air—is self-ventilating.

To prevent the entry of foul air into a house, every stack vent, whether it runs up through the roof or up an outside wall, should rise to a point that is not less than 1 metre above and 3 metres to the side of any window or opening; this will ensure that foul gases cannot enter.

The existing stack vent will ventilate any new branch soil or waste pipes leading into it unless the trap is further than the recommended distance from the main stack. The recommended distances are 6 metres for a W.C.; 2.3 metres for baths, sinks and showers; and 1.7 metres for basins and bidets. If a new fixture is farther than the recommended distance from the stack, you will have to provide for additional ventilation. In Australia and New Zealand this

work must be done by a licensed plumber.

The simplest method of doing this is to install an anti-siphon valve near the fixture *(below)*, but before doing this, first check with your local authority that they are allowed in your area.

An alternative means is to install secondary ventilation. Pipework for this can either run upwards from the new branch pipe through the roof or a wall, or it can cross-ventilate to the existing vent stack in the attic or roof space *(opposite page, above)*. Cross-ventilation is often the easier solution, as it avoids cutting a hole through the roof or wall. In some situations, it is possible to vent two or more new fixtures with one new vent line *(opposite page, below)*, but soil and waste vents should never be combined.

A cross-ventilating pipe should always slant up towards the main stack, and must join it above the overflow level of the highest fixture discharging into it.

The diameter of the vent pipe will be 32, 40 or 50 mm, depending on the size of the pipe it is venting: a discharge pipe less than 75 mm needs a vent at least two-thirds the size of its diameter, while one over 75 mm will require a 50 mm vent.

Because it is important to keep the air flowing at a stack vent outlet, fit a wire balloon or plastic cap to prevent it blocking up and to stop birds choosing it as a warm and comfortable spot for their nests.

A Shortcut to Additional Venting

An anti-siphon valve. An anti-siphon valve, fitted either to a horizontal waste pipe *(below)* or a vertical waste pipe *(inset)*, must be upright and connected to the waste pipe within 300 mm of the trap crown. Depending on the model, the valve can either be solvent-welded or push-fitted into a swept tee installed in the waste pipe, or screwed into a special fitting supplied with the valve. As an anti-siphon valve for a W.C. must be above the level of the pan rim, you will have to install a short length of vertical pipe into the swept tee to raise the valve.

Under normal conditions, the valve remains closed to the outside air, but if the volume of water flowing through the pipe leaves a negative pressure behind it, so creating a vacuum between itself and the trap, the valve will open to restore atmospheric pressure.

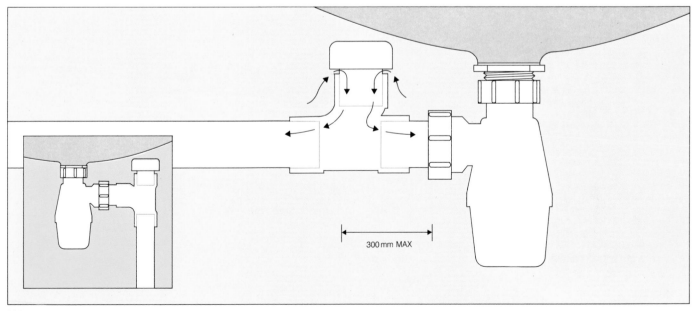

300 mm MAX

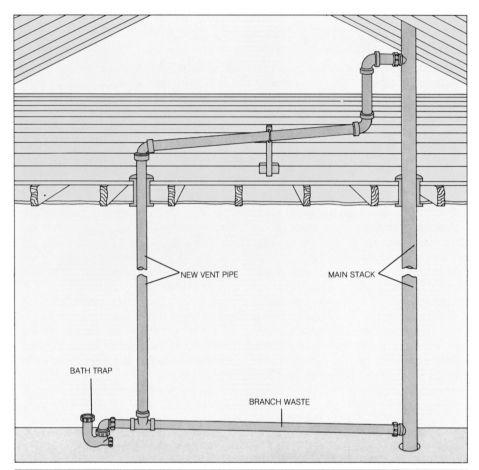

Cross-Ventilating for New Fixtures

A vent for a single fixture. Install a swept tee or boss connector in the branch pipe, between 75 and 300 mm from the crown of the bath trap. Drop a plumb line from the ceiling into the centre of the boss or tee, and cut a hole in the ceiling *(page 96)*. Cut a length of pipe long enough to reach from the branch pipe and extend 300 mm into the attic, and push the top end through the hole before securing the lower end to the boss or tee.

Use 92½-degree bend fittings and further lengths of pipe to slope the new vent line up to the stack, and make the final join to the stack with a boss connector. If you find that the route of the vent line prevents it from being bracketed against a wall in the roof space or attic, nail timber uprights to the floorboards or joists and fix brackets to them.

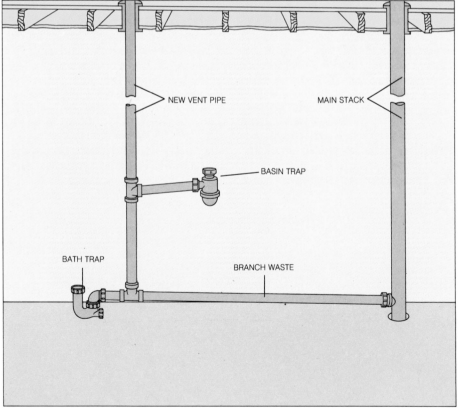

A single vent for two fixtures. Install a swept tee in the branch waste pipe and drop a plumb line from the ceiling to the centre of the tee outlet. Mark the path of the plumb line on the wall. Calculate the fall line *(page 102)* from the basin trap to the vertical path you have just marked: where they meet will be the position of the swept tee connecting the basin waste to the new vertical pipe. Install a suitable length of pipe to connect the two swept tees, and run the vent line up through the ceiling to the main stack *(left)*.

Getting the Water to the Fixtures: the Supply System

Supplying a bathroom with hot and cold water is usually much easier than installing pipes for soil and waste. The supply lines need not be pitched, because the water in them is under pressure, and will consequently move in any direction. The pipes themselves are much smaller and are therefore easier to fit round obstacles, or disguise if unsightly.

Choose copper or cPVC pipes and fittings, providing your local authority permits their use. If your existing supply pipes are in some other material, you will need to use transition fittings *(page 114)* to connect the old material to the new. In the case of galvanized steel, use cPVC rather than copper: electrolytic action can occur between galvanized steel and copper, causing corrosion of the zinc coating on the inner surface of the steel pipe, and ultimately leading to corrosion of the steel itself.

The size of pipe used depends on the function of the supply line and the number of fittings attached to it. The most common sizes are 28 mm, usually used to lead from the cistern if the room to be supplied is more than 6 metres away from it; 22 mm, used to supply baths, or a kitchen sink if you are installing appliances such as a dishwasher and washing machine as well; and 15 mm for all other fittings.

Always observe two basic rules. First, never tap into a line which is smaller than the new branch line. If existing pipes are too small, install new parallel supply lines. In an indirect system, you may be able to connect additional fixtures directly to the rising main, for example for a downstairs W.C. and washbasin, but always check with your local water authority first. Second, wherever possible use a long-radius bend rather than an elbow joint if a supply pipe has to change direction. The frictional resistance which is created by an elbow fitting has the same effect on the flow of water as increasing the length of the pipe by 1 metre would have.

To avoid the danger of scalding, a shower must always be connected directly to the cold water cistern, which has a constant water pressure, rather than to an existing cold water supply pipe; cold water pressure can be suddenly reduced if any other appliances on the same supply pipe are being used at the same time.

Once you have decided on your route, shut off the water supply to those pipes to which new ones will be connected. In an indirect system, close the service stop valves on the cold water distribution and the cold feed leading from the cistern to the hot water cylinder. If you do not have service stop valves, drain the whole system. Close the main stop tap and, starting at the top of the house, open all the taps and flush all the W.C.s. Finally, open the drain cock on the rising main.

New hot and cold lines should be run parallel to each other and about 150 mm apart. Position the cold water pipe below the hot water pipe, and insulate both pipes if they will run through unheated areas. To connect new and old copper pipes, use either a non-manipulative compression joint *(opposite page, below)* or a soldered capillary joint *(page 110, above)*. Compression fittings are more expensive, but they have the advantage of being quicker and easier to assemble than soldered fittings.

Copper has the additional advantage that it can be bent, which avoids the need for a series of elbow joints when fitting round obstacles or turning corners. Where new copper pipes are to run along a wall in the same plane as existing ones, a passover *(pages 110–111)* will enable both new pipes to run the same bracket distance from the wall, creating a neater finish.

Piping made of cPVC is often chosen in preference to copper, partly because it is less expensive. Unlike copper, cPVC cannot be bent, but its solvent cement welded joints make it an easily installed and convenient material to use. Since cPVC has not long been in use for supply lines, you will nearly always be connecting to another material, and therefore will have to use an adapter fitting *(page 112)*.

All new branch lines should be fitted with a stop valve to enable you to isolate individual sections of the branch for any future repairs or alterations. On straight sections of pipe, this can either be a gate or screw-down stop valve; do not use an anti-return stop valve, except on mains cold water supplies. Where pipes are to join an appliance at right angles to the wall, use angled stop valves *(page 112)*. It is compulsory to fit drain valves *(page 112)* on any new installation which cannot be drained from the existing system.

When you have completed an installation, test the new lines for leaks. Cap the ends of the lines *(page 91)*, then open the stop valves in the new supply branches and fill the lines with water. Wait an hour before concealing the pipes or mounting fixtures. If leaks do occur, drain the branch or system again and then proceed to reconnect the defective joints.

In Australia and New Zealand a licensed plumber will do these installations following the same principles described above.

Tapping a Copper Pipe

Marking the tube stops. Shut off the water supply and drain the branch you wish to tap. Hold the tee fitting upright against the supply pipe at the point where you are going to insert it, and mark the two tube stops of the tee on the pipe. Using a hacksaw, cut through at right angles to the pipe at both these points *(inset)*.

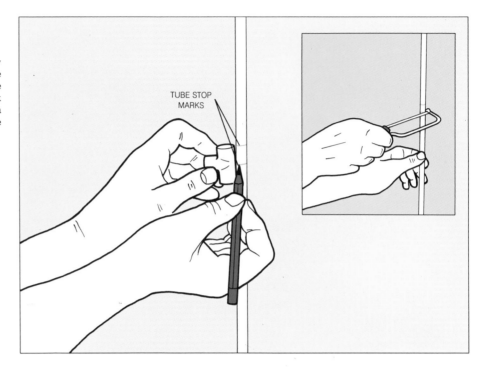

TUBE STOP MARKS

Connecting the Pipes: Copper Compression Joints

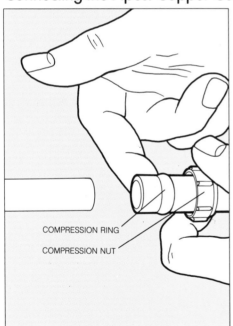

COMPRESSION RING

COMPRESSION NUT

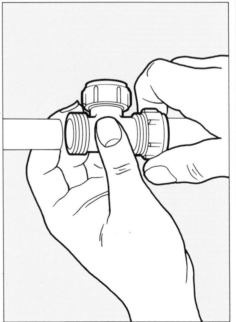

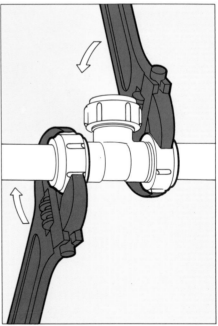

1 Applying jointing compound. Smooth any rough edges on the pipe using a file and sandpaper. Separate the two ends of the pipe. Slide a compression nut, followed by a compression ring, on to the end of one of the pipes. Smear jointing compound on to the ring to ensure that the joint is watertight. Make sure that the jointing compound does not go inside the pipe or on the screw threads of the nut, where it might make the joint difficult to dismantle.

2 Fitting the tee joint. Slip the end of the tee joint over the compression ring. Push it down as far as it will go, and screw the compression nut on to the tee joint by hand. Put the second nut and ring on to the other end of the pipe, smear it with jointing compound as before, and screw the nut on to the fitting.

3 Tightening the nuts. Using a pair of spanners or wrenches, turn the two nuts carefully in opposite directions. It is important not to overtighten them, as this can cause distortion of the compression rings, which can lead to leaks. For most pipe sizes, a single complete turn of the spanner is sufficient, and pipes with a larger diameter or thinner walls will need even less.

Capillary Joints

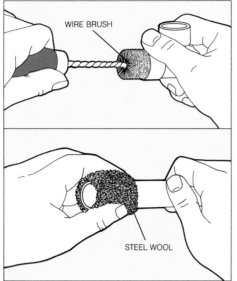

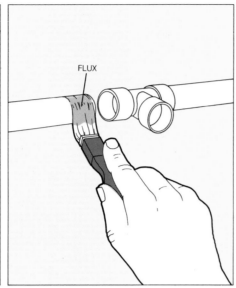

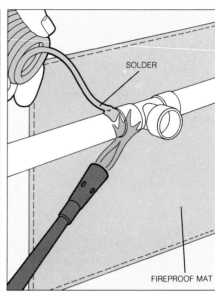

1 Cleaning the pipe. To ensure that the melted solder will flow evenly and adhere properly, scour the inner surfaces of the joint with a wire brush. Burnish the end of the pipe with emery cloth or steel wool, and do not touch either surface after cleaning. Even a fingerprint will weaken the joint.

2 Preparing the joint for soldering. Coat both the cleaned surfaces with a light cover of flux. Assemble the joint, twisting the pipe to distribute the flux evenly. Use a fireproof mat behind the joint to protect the surface while soldering. Light the torch and play the flame over the fitting and surrounding pipe, heating them as evenly as possible.

3 Soldering the joint. Touch the solder to both the pipe and the fitting. When it melts, the joint is ready for soldering; do not heat further, or the flux will burn off. The solder should melt only by contact with the pipe, and not by the flame. If this fails to happen, play the flame on the joint again to reheat it. When the temperature of the joint is correct, molten solder will be drawn by capillary action into the fitting to seal the connection. Continue feeding solder until the joint is completed. You will need a length of solder equal to the diameter of the pipe.

Making a Passover

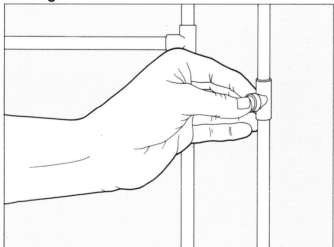

1 Angling the tee. Connect one new supply pipe to the existing pipe with a tee. Insert—but do not secure—a second tee into the other existing supply pipe so that the horizontal exit line will clear the first supply pipe.

2 Making the first bend. Take a length of copper tubing about 200 mm longer than the distance from the tee to the fitting and insert a bending spring into one end. (The extra length is needed to give the spring leverage.) Measure the distance between the centre of the two vertical supply pipes, add 200 mm and mark this distance on the pipe, measuring from one end. Place a pad between your knee and the pipe and form a bend; the centre should be at the mark you have made.

3 Calculating the passover size. Slip a piece of scrap pipe into the tee and measure from the centre of the first supply pipe to the centre of the scrap pipe *(below)*. Lay the bent pipe on the floor, spring still in it, against a straightedge. Measure the same distance from the straightedge to the pipe, below the bend, and mark the pipe *(inset)*.

4 Making the second bend. At this second point you have marked, bend the pipe again to form the other side of the passover curve. Hold the bent pipe as close as possible to its final position, and make any further adjustments to the curve.

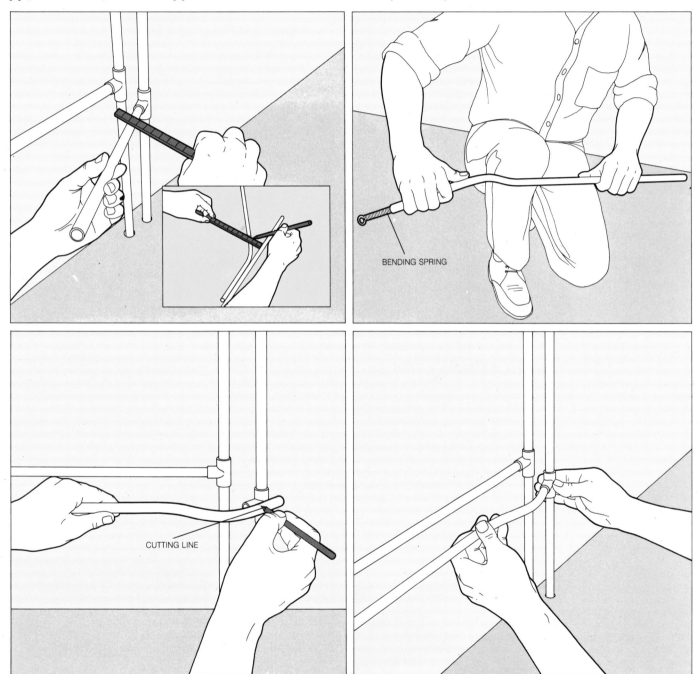

BENDING SPRING

CUTTING LINE

5 Adjusting the length. Remove the bending spring and cut off the excess 200 mm length of pipe above the curve. To do this, hold the end of the bent pipe alongside the tee and carefully mark where to cut the pipe so that it will fit nicely into the tee *(above)*.

6 Completing the passover. Cut the pipe and put the tee in position in the supply pipe. Slip the bent pipe into the tee and make any final adjustments to length before soldering or tightening the compression fitting.

Connecting cPVC to Copper Pipes

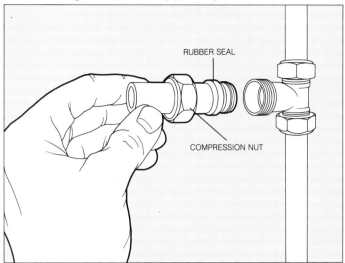

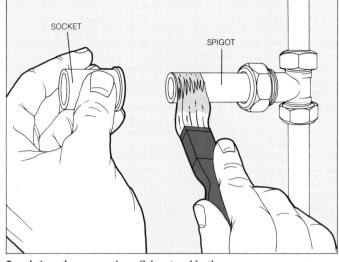

1 Inserting the adapter. Insert a tee compression fitting *(page 109)* into the existing supply pipe. Remove the compression nut from the tee branch and discard the compression ring. Slip the compression nut over the spigot of the adapter. Push the end with the rubber seal into the compression fitting and tighten the nut.

2 Completing the connection. Solvent-weld the socket on to the spigot end of the adapter and then the new supply pipe into the other end of the socket. Before welding, remove all swarf with a file, and wipe the pipe and adapter surfaces with solvent cleaner. Apply solvent cement liberally to the spigot and pipe outer surfaces, taking special care not to miss the spigot rim. Apply less inside the socket. Assemble the joint quickly, and do not wipe off any surplus cement.

Installing Valves

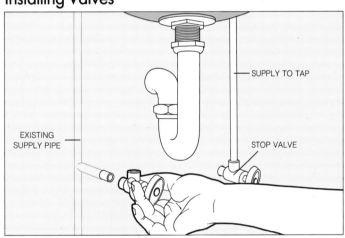

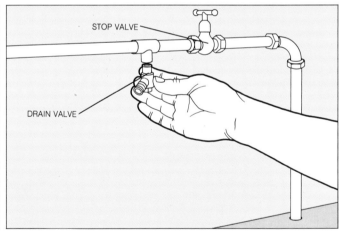

An angled stop-valve. In a case where a pipe comes through a wall from behind to an individual fixture, it is both convenient and economical to fit an angled stop-valve *(above)*. This will enable you to isolate the fixture for future repairs or alterations. It also saves having to use an additional elbow fixture, and therefore reduces friction in the pipe. The angled stop-valve is only available in cPVC and is fitted in the same way as for cPVC pipes *(above, right)*, after the plumbing work installed so far has been checked for leaks. All that is needed to complete the installation is a short length of pipe from the stop valves to the taps *(page 119)*.

A drain valve. When installing a new water supply, it is compulsory in the U.K. to make sure that all the pipes can be drained at the lowest point of the flow. If new installations cannot be drained from the existing system, you must decide on the most convenient place to locate a new drain valve. Remember that drain valves need to be easily accessible. The best place to fit a new valve is at the lowest point on the pipe as close as possible to the fixture, where you can conceal it with a floorboard or removable panel if necessary. The simplest and most versatile type of drain valve is one which can be soldered into any capillary tee fitting *(page 110)*.

Increasing the Flow of Water

Maintaining an adequate flow of water through the supply pipes is most important for a satisfactory plumbing system. If the flow is restricted, you can ascertain the cause and find a solution; for example, you can improve the performance of a shower by boosting the flow. When adding on new fixtures you should ensure a sufficient water flow to them.

If water just barely trickles from one tap, the problem may be nothing more than a clogged spout or seized washer. But if trickles are all you get at any fixture in the bathroom or kitchen, the cause may be hard to find. It can be as simple as a main stop valve mistakenly left half closed. More often, the problem is due to one of two causes. The first is outside the house: inadequate pressure in the mains supply, which you can do nothing about; the second is inside the house: restricted flow due either to blockages in pipes and fittings, or to faults in the design and installation of the supply system, which you can take steps to remedy.

First check taps, stop valves and ball valves for blockages, and if necessary clean the bodies and seats *(page 114)*. If this does not improve the flow, take flow tests *(chart, right)* to establish where the problem is located in the pipework.

Check pipes for blockages by looking for signs of rust, corrosion and furring. Rust usually attacks galvanized steel piping, particularly if it is connected to copper. Look out for stains on fixtures below tap spouts or a brownish flow from a tap if it has not been used for some time. Furring occurs where the water supply is hard and affects hot water fittings and pipes more seriously than cold water ones. Check for white, scaly deposits round tap spouts. If you suspect the pipe is clogged, open it up between unions or fittings, and replace the blocked section with new copper or cPVC tubing *(page 114)*.

Obstructed pipes that do not show signs of corrosion or furring may be blocked by silt or other debris that has been washed down from the cold water cistern. Attach a hose to the draintap at the lowest point in the affected pipe and allow the water to run until it is clear.

When the fittings and pipes do not seem to be blocked, check for faults in the installation and design of the system. An easily remedied fault may lie with stop valves on low pressure supplies. In the U.K. screwdown stop taps may be replaced with gate valves which offer less restriction to flow *(page 114)*.

Airlocks, due to poorly planned pipework, can also reduce the flow of water and even stop it altogether. This can often be cured by attaching one end of a hose to the affected tap and the other to a mains cold water tap and turning on both taps. If the airlocks recur, ask a plumber to check the design of the system.

Restricted flow can also be caused by undersized pipes. Check if the problem area is served by small diameter pipes travelling a long distance and serving several fixtures or including a large number of bends—every elbow turn in a 15 or 22 mm pipe has the same effect on the flow as adding one metre to the length of the pipe. The only solution is to replace the run with larger diameter pipes.

When installing new fixtures, you can avoid the risk of overburdening the existing supply lines—particularly if they already include long tortuous runs serving many fixtures—by making parallel supplies instead *(page 115)*. Taking the new supplies as close to the water sources as possible will ensure a good volume of flow to the new fixtures.

Showers are often a problem if only a weak dribble comes from the shower head rather than a powerful spray. This is because there is not enough distance between the base of the cold water cistern and the shower head, and therefore not enough pressure to create a powerful flow. The minimum distance should be 1 metre, and the higher the cistern the better the spray. One solution, if your roof space allows it, is to raise the cistern by making a platform and lengthening the connecting pipework. Another, simpler solution is to install a shower pump *(page 115)* which will boost the pressure, so that the shower head can even be placed above the level of the base of the cold water cistern, as long as the pump is below it.

Minimum Flow Rates

Fixture	Litres per minute
Basin	9
Bath	18
Shower	7.2
W.C. cistern	7.2
Sink	12

Taking flow tests. These minimum satisfactory flow rates for a variety of fixtures, based on plumbing codes, can help you to locate badly clogged branch pipes or warn you that the system is inadequate. At each fixture use a stop watch to measure the time taken to fill a one-litre jug. Divide the number of seconds into 60 to calculate the flow in litres per minute. If only one or two fixtures give readings close to or lower than the chart minimums, check taps and pipes for blockages. If all the readings are low and blockages have been ruled out, the pipes should be replaced with ones of a larger diameter.

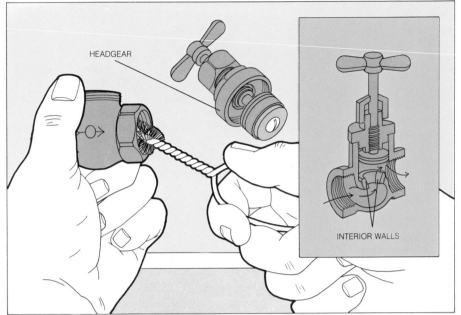

HEADGEAR

INTERIOR WALLS

Clearing the Passages Through Valves and Pipes

Cleaning a screw-down stop valve. To get the valve apart, first close the nearest valve on the inlet side and drain water from the first tap beyond the discharge side. Then, if the pipework is steel, open the pipe at a nearby union and unscrew the valve. If the valve is close to a joist or wall, you may have to unscrew the headgear in order to rotate the valve body; otherwise, separate the headgear from the body at a workbench.

For copper pipework, either undo the compression fittings or, if the stop valve is soldered in, cut the pipe on either side of it.

Soak the stop valve in spirit of salts (a hydrochloric acid solution) for a few minutes to dissolve the mineral deposits. Rinse it thoroughly in cold water and, with a stiff wire brush, loosen and remove stubborn particles lodged against the interior walls. Wear rubber gloves and goggles.

When you reinstall the valve make sure the arrow on the body points in the direction of the water flow *(inset)*.

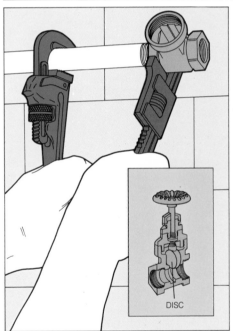

DISC

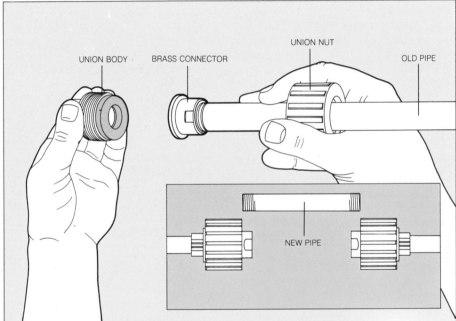

UNION BODY   BRASS CONNECTOR   UNION NUT   OLD PIPE

NEW PIPE

Installing a gate valve. If a screw-down stop valve has been fitted on low pressure supply pipes—the distribution pipes from the cold water cistern or the hot water cylinder, for example—replace it with a gate valve, using a wrench to hold the pipe and a toothless adjustable spanner to work the valve. A stop valve slows water by channelling it through an S-shaped path, while a gate valve's base houses a vertical disc that rises to allow a direct passage *(inset)* with less pressure loss. Before starting work, shut off the mains water stop valve and drain the system by opening the taps at each fixture and draining water from the drain taps situated at the lowest points of the hot and cold water pipes. To avoid mineral build-up in the headgear, install the valve with the handle upwards or sideways.

Replacing clogged pipes. Use two transition fittings to join a replacement section of copper or cPVC tubing to galvanized pipe. First unscrew the affected section from between the two nearest fittings and replace any rusted fittings—elbows or tees—with new galvanized fittings. Slip the union nut of one of the connectors over the steel pipe, and wrap PTFE tape round the pipe thread (if you use a male connector, wrap

the tape around its thread). Tighten the brass connector on to the taped thread with a spanner. Fit another transition fitting to the other section of galvanized pipe. Measure the distance between the two tube stops and cut a pipe to this length. Undo the two union nuts and remove the union bodies. Attach a union body to each end of the replacement pipe, soldering copper pipes and solvent welding cPVC; reassemble the fittings.

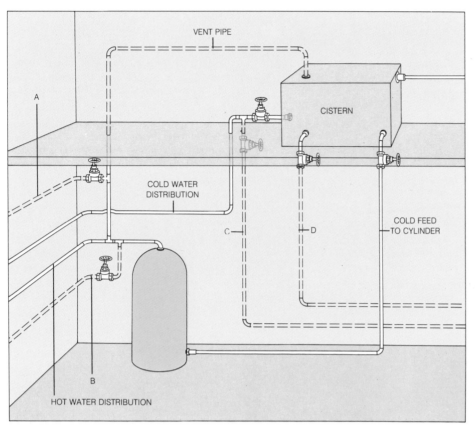

Improving the Water Flow for New Fixtures

Installing parallel supplies. A parallel hot water supply can either be taken from any section of the vent pipe below the base of the cold water cistern (A), or from the hot water distribution pipe as near to the hot water cylinder as possible (B).

A parallel cold water supply can either be taken from the cold water distribution pipe (C), or directly from the cistern (D). If your cold water comes direct from the mains, take the parallel supply as close to where the mains enter the house as possible. Never take a new cold water supply from the cold feed to the hot water cylinder or from a cold feed to a shower.

To install a parallel line, tee into the existing pipe with a new one of the same diameter, using a capillary or compression fitting *(pages 109–110)*.

Make the route of the parallel supply to the fixtures as direct as possible, and use long radius bend fittings rather than sharp elbow turns. If you are taking a new line from the cistern, drill a hole in the side of the cistern and use a special fitting known as a tank connector, to which the new pipe can be attached. Any new outlets in the cistern should be at least 50 mm above the bottom to prevent silt going down the new pipe. Install a stop valve *(page 112)* just after the tee fitting or tank connector.

Boosting the Pressure for a Shower

Installing a shower pump. Before putting in a shower pump, check that the distance between the cold water cistern and the proposed pump location meets the manufacturer's requirements.

Lead in 1 mm^2 earthed cable to the location of the pump via a double-pole switched spur box which must be positioned out of reach of the shower user. Remove the pump cover and mount the pump on the wall with the screws provided. Make the wiring connections according to the manufacturer's instructions. Replace the cover.

Unscrew the shower hose from the bath mixer taps and secure it to the right-hand spigot on the pump base. Then connect the flexible hose supplied with the pump between the left-hand pump spigot and the bath mixer taps.

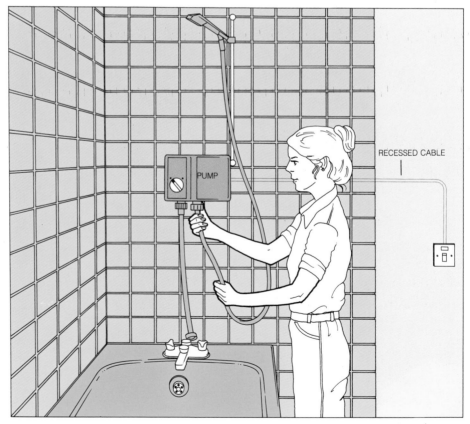

The Final Step: Installing the Fixtures

Once the pipes have been run to the desired location, the installation of most new baths, basins and W.C.s simply reverses the procedures used to remove the old ones (*pages 88–91*). For ease of assembly, however, taps, waste fittings and traps should be fitted before the fixtures are secured in their final location and connected to their supply, waste and soil pipes.

Most basins and baths are supplied with tap holes, but some basins have punched holes that can be knocked out to suit the tap assembly, depending on whether it is a one, two or three-hole type. All tap assemblies, including mixer taps with small-bore tube tails in place of the conventional threaded tails, are secured to the fixture with a back nut (*below*).

Strainers for waste fittings either form an integral part of the fitting (*opposite page, top left*) or are secured to the fitting with a screw (*opposite page, top right*). The integral fitting shown opposite has a slot to receive an in-built overflow channel. Fixtures that require a separate overflow channel—all baths, and some basins and bidets—must be fitted with a combined waste and overflow assembly (*opposite page, below*). For baths, use a special combined assembly which incorporates a trap;

this takes up less room and avoids the necessity of cutting a hole in the floor to accommodate a separate trap.

A basin or bidet pop-up plug is operated by two interlocking rods (*page 118, above*). A bath pop-up resembles a combined waste and overflow assembly but also incorporates a cable linking the plug to a control knob on the front of the overflow hole (*page 118, below*).

Where a watertight seal is needed—such as under strainer and waste flanges—use mastic or a mixture of putty and jointing paste; on threaded connections that are not sealed by a washer or compression ring, use a pipe-joint compound or PTFE tape. After completing an installation, check your work by turning on the water and searching for leaks with your fingers as well as your eyes.

With the fitting installed and the fixtures secured in their planned positions, make any necessary final adjustments to the length of the supply, waste and soil pipes. Most connections to pipes or stop valves require little more than the tightening of nuts, but take care not to damage any of the parts by overtightening—always hand-tighten the nuts first, then make an extra quarter turn with a wrench.

Taps with threaded tails are joined to stop valves with a short length of small-bore tube (*page 119, top left*); the small-bore tube tails of mixer taps are connected directly to the stop valves (*page 119, top right*). Wall-mounted taps and recessed shower assemblies require special care (*page 119, below*); the bodies of the fittings must be positioned in the wall very accurately so that the final connections are flush with the finished wall.

While most fixtures are installed after floors and walls are finished, baths should go in before, particularly if they have wall supports that must be hidden by the decorative finish (*page 101*).

Once you have fitted a tee joint into the soil stack, the installation of a new W.C. (*pages 120–121*) is straightforward. Most parts are supplied by the manufacturer but you must provide a connector to join the toilet pan to the branch waste, two 15 mm tap washers, and 60 mm No. 12 brass countersunk wood screws which will be used to secure the pan to the floor and the cistern to the wall.

In Australia and New Zealand (where this work must be done by a licensed plumber), some fittings may differ in design from those shown here.

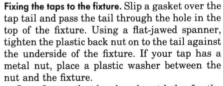

Fixing the taps to the fixture. Slip a gasket over the tap tail and pass the tail through the hole in the top of the fixture. Using a flat-jawed spanner, tighten the plastic back nut on to the tail against the underside of the fixture. If your tap has a metal nut, place a plastic washer between the nut and the fixture.

On a fixture that has knock-out holes for the taps instead of ready-made holes, tape over the holes you will be using and knock them out with the ball end of a ball-pein hammer.

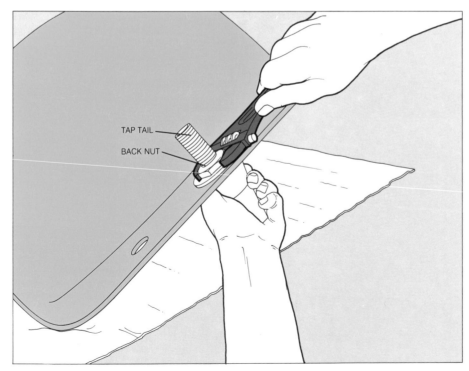

TAP TAIL

BACK NUT

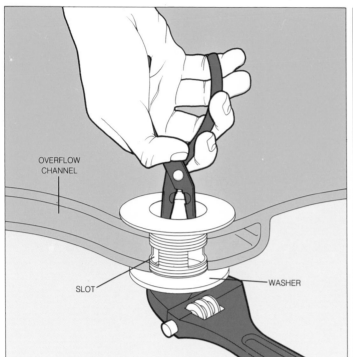

Installing an integral waste. Insert the waste fitting in the outlet hole of the fixture. If the fixture has an integral overflow channel, use a slotted waste, as shown above. Place the washer and the back nut over the threaded tail. Use a pair of long-nosed pliers inserted into the strainer slots to prevent the fitting from turning as you tighten the back nut with a flat-jawed spanner.

Fitting a screw-down waste. Put the strainer over the outlet hole. Place the washer on the waste tail and align them with the outlet hole. Thread the screw through the centre of the strainer and then use a screwdriver to secure it firmly to the waste tail *(above)*.

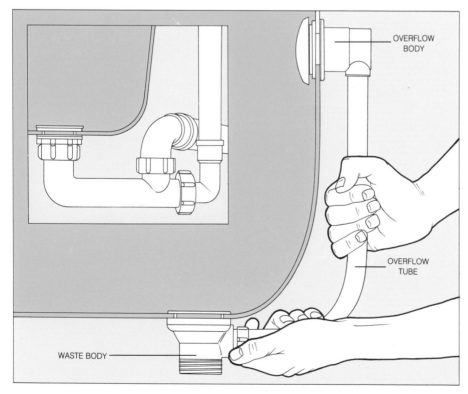

Installing a combined waste and overflow. Fit the strainer and waste body to the fixture *(above, right)*, then push the overflow front face through the overflow hole and screw it on to the threaded body. Insert the bottom end of the overflow tube in the socket in the waste body and tighten the nut over the compression ring. On a bath waste fitting incorporating overflow and trap *(inset)*, the bottom of the overflow tube connects into the back of the trap instead of into the waste body.

Installing a Basin Pop-Up

Assembling the unit. Slip the waste through the basin outlet, screw the waste body to it and drop the plug into the waste. By hand, adjust the retaining nut that secures the pivot rod to the waste body, so that the rod moves up and down easily on its ball-bearing. Slip the pivot rod through the retaining screw clip on the lift rod, positioning the two rods at right angles to each other. Tighten the retaining screw with a pair of mole grips until the rods are firmly held together. Test the pop-up mechanism by lifting the rod up so that the plug drops down into the waste. If the plug does not lie flush with the waste flange, remove the plug, move the adjusting screw up the thread a few millimetres *(inset)*, and secure it with the locking collar. Replace the plug and test again.

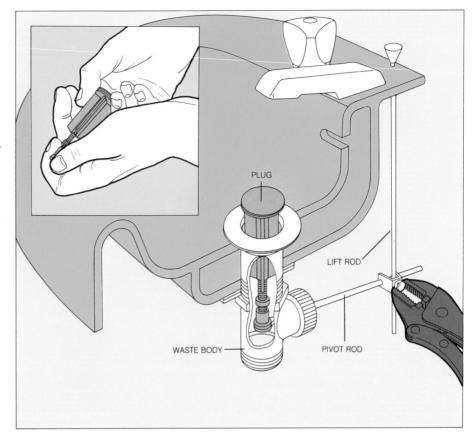

A Pop-Up for a Bath

Fitting the pop-up. Install the waste and overflow fittings as described on page 117, below; the type shown here has a rigid overflow pipe which is adjusted to the bath height by sliding the lower half up or down in the collar *(right)*. Slip the star washer on to the overflow grid, and screw the grid on to the spindle. Slide the front face on to the spindle with its access hole facing downwards, then secure the face to the spindle with the retaining screw. Insert the pop-up plug into the waste and test the mechanism: turning the front face anticlockwise pulls up the cable and allows the plug to drop down, sealing the outlet. If necessary, adjust the plug as for a basin.

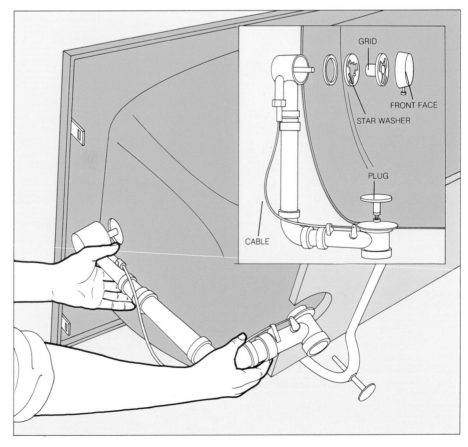

Connecting Taps to Stop Valves

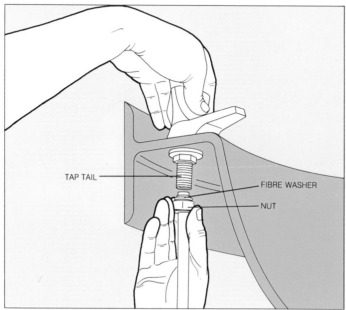

TAP TAIL

FIBRE WASHER

NUT

A threaded tail. Measure the distance between the threaded tail of the tap and the stop valve, and cut a length of small-bore tube to fit. Solder or solvent-weld a connector fitting to one end of the tube, and screw the connector nut on to the threaded tail of the tap *(above)*. Attach the bottom end of the tube to the stop valve with a compression fitting.

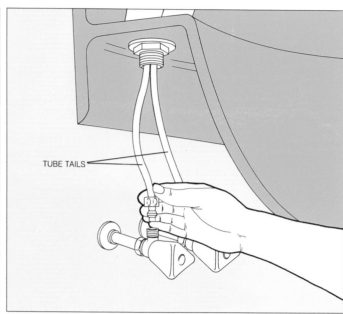

TUBE TAILS

Mixer tap tube tails. Cut the tube tails of the mixer tap to the required length to join them to the stop valves. Slip a compression ring and nut over the end of one of the tails, and screw the nut on to the stop valve. Attach the second tail to the other stop valve in the same way. Tighten the nuts with a wrench or spanner.

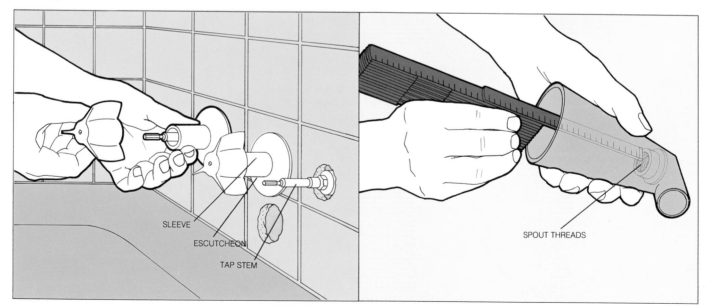

SLEEVE

ESCUTCHEON

TAP STEM

SPOUT THREADS

Wall-mounted fittings. To install certain tap or diverter-valve handles, slide escutcheons and sleeves on to the protruding stems *(above, left)* before screwing on the handles. For other types of handles, including single-lever controls, follow the manufacturer's instructions. Before mounting the spout, measure from the face of the elbow fitting behind the wall to the face of the wall, add the distance from the threads in the spout to the end of the spout, plus another 20 mm *(above, right)*. Cut a brass or galvanized steel nipple to this length and apply PTFE tape to the thread at one end of the nipple. Using a wrench, tighten the taped end of the nipple on to the elbow fitting. Apply PTFE tape to the protruding thread of the nipple and screw on the spout as tightly as possible with your hands.

To install a shower arm, remove the nipple from the supply pipe. Apply PTFE tape to the threads of the arm, place the escutcheon over the arm and screw the arm to the pipe by hand.

Hooking up a W.C.

1 **Measuring for the soil pipe.** Position the W.C. pan in its planned location and push a PVC pan connector on to its waste outlet. Remove the panelling from around the main stack, calculate the fall line from the pan connector *(page 102)*, and fit a tee connector in the stack *(page 104)*. Measure the distance between the tube stop in the pan connector and the stop in the tee connector in the main stack *(right)*, then cut a 100 mm PVC soil pipe to this length. Smooth and chamfer the ends of the soil pipe with a coarse file.

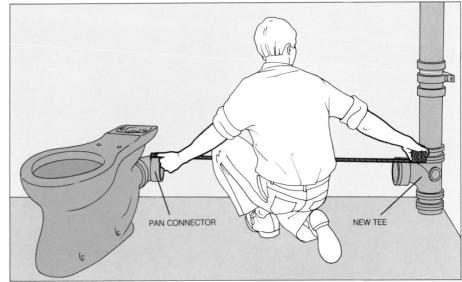

PAN CONNECTOR   NEW TEE

2 **Attaching the soil pipe.** Move the W.C. pan aside and remove the pan connector. Using solvent cement, secure one end of the soil pipe to the pan connector and the other end to the tee connector in the main stack. Move the W.C. pan back into its planned location, pushing the pan outlet into the pan connector.

SOIL PIPE

3 **Securing the cistern to the pan.** With the cistern resting on the floor, assemble the fittings according to the manufacturer's instructions. Lift the cistern on to the rear of the pan *(right)*, ensuring that the bolts protruding from the bottom of the cistern fall through the corresponding holes in the pan. Screw the washers and wing nuts provided by the manufacturer on to the bolts to secure the cistern to the pan *(inset)*.

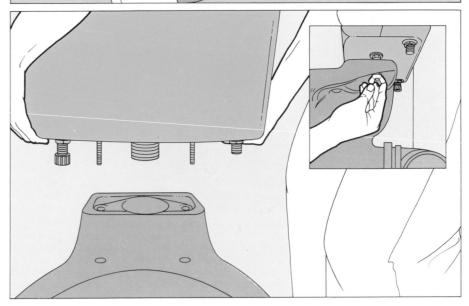

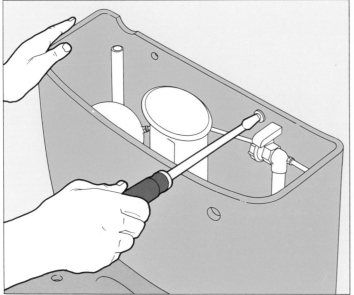

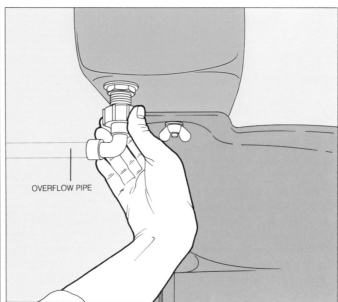

4 **Fixing the cistern to the wall.** If necessary, move the pan slightly until the back of the cistern is resting squarely against the wall. Through the two holes in the back of the cistern, drill holes in the wall; insert plugs in the holes, place 15 mm tap washers under the heads of two 60 mm No. 12 brass countersunk wood screws, and screw the cistern to the wall (*above*). Then secure the pan to the floor with similar screws.

5 **Fitting the overflow pipe.** If the W.C. backs on to an outside wall, drill a hole through the wall close to the overflow outlet, using a power drill and a long masonry bit. Cut a length of pipe to extend at least 100 mm outside the wall, then attach it to the cistern outlet with a compression elbow fitting (*above*). Make good the hole in the wall. On a W.C. backing on to an inside wall, connect the cistern overflow outlet to a pipe run that extends to the nearest convenient outside wall.

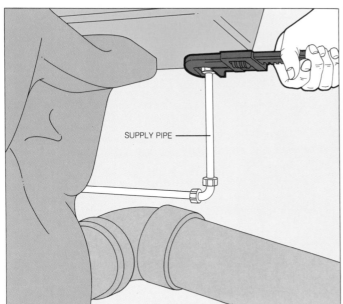

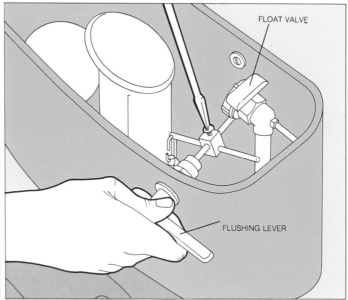

6 **Connecting the supply pipe.** Use compression tee and elbow fittings to lead new pipework from an existing supply pipe to the threaded water inlet pipe at the side or, as here, at the base of the cistern. Join the end of the new supply pipe to the cistern inlet with a tap connector.

7 **Completing the installation.** Assemble the flushing arm mechanism inside the cistern according to the manufacturer's instructions. Fit the flushing lever on to the outside of the cistern and adjust its alignment with the flushing arm. Tighten the retaining screw (*above*). Turn on the water supply. If necessary, adjust the regulator on the float valve so that the water level corresponds with the level line marked inside the cistern.

Special Fittings for Kitchen Sinks

Among the wide range of specialized fittings and labour-saving appliances for kitchens that are now available, there are many that can easily be installed by the amateur, unless not permitted by local plumbing regulations. Their designs vary widely, but their plumbing-in procedures follow the same basic pattern.

A spray for rinsing dishes or washing vegetables is connected in the same way as the supply pipes to a compatible tap *(below)*. Taps themselves vary widely in their mode of operation, and you should consider your requirements carefully before choosing among them. For a double sink, install a mixer tap with a swivelling arm; the tap handles may be either spaced apart and have conventional threaded tails or set into the arm base and have small-bore tube tails. A reverse-pressure tap—which is usually known by its trade name, Supatap—is turned on and off by revolving the tap nozzle; it can be disassembled for replacing the washer without having to shut off the water supply, but requires a special connector if a hose is attached for filling a washing machine or garden use. Single-lever mixer taps can be turned on and off and adjusted for temperature with one hand, but automatically shut off when the lever is released.

Double sinks are available in a range of sizes and depths, and are no more difficult to plumb in than a single sink: a single trap is fitted beneath the sink nearer the waste outlet, and a double sink set accommodates the waste pipe from the second sink *(opposite page, above)*. The sinks are often different depths, with one shallow sink for rinsing dishes and the other deep enough for washing large pieces of kitchen equipment such as pans and oven shelves; sometimes the sink is fitted with a removable chopping board that provides extra work space when the sink is not being used. If the sink has no punched or knock-out holes for taps, use a hole saw to cut out holes in the worktop surface.

A special washing machine trap fitted to a sink waste *(opposite page, below)* simplifies the task of plumbing in a washing machine, dishwasher or any other appliance whose waste pipe must accommodate an air gap to maintain atmospheric pressure and prevent the back-siphonage of waste water. This fitting avoids the need to install an open standpipe with its own trap and separate waste pipe. To maintain the necessary air gap and thereby avoid back-siphonage of waste water, the sink plug must not be inserted in the waste while the washing machine is being used.

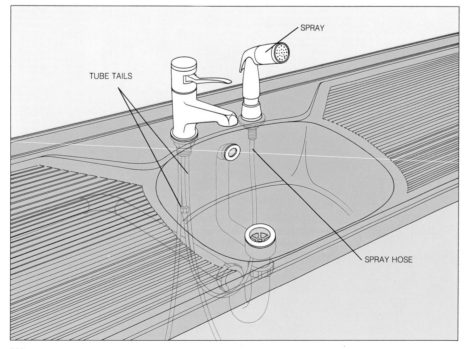

Fitting a spray rinse. Slip rubber gaskets over the mixer tap and spray rinse tails or apply a bead of mastic jointing compound. Slide the tails through the holes in the sink or worktop. Secure the tap and spray rinse to the worktop with the washers and back-nuts provided, as described on page 116. Connect the tube inlet tails of the mixer tap to the shut-off valves as described on page 119, top right. Connect the free end of the spray hose to the third tube tail with an adapter fitting.

SPRAY

TUBE TAILS

SPRAY HOSE

A waste fitting for a double sink. Attach combined waste and overflow fittings to both sinks as described on page 117. Secure a double sink set to the wastes of both sinks with the compression nuts provided, ensuring that the branch of the sink set is secured to the waste farthest away from the waste outlet. Connect a P-trap to the bottom outlet of the sink set and to the drain pipe with the compression nuts provided.

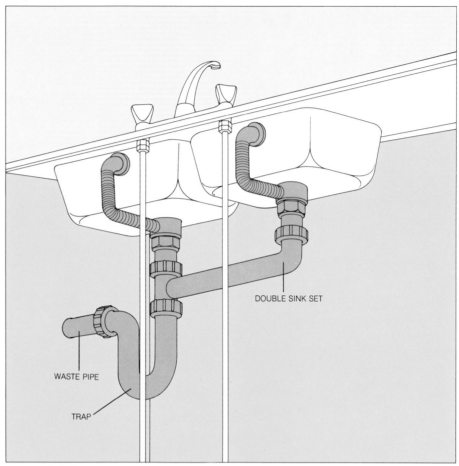

WASTE PIPE

TRAP

DOUBLE SINK SET

A washing machine trap. Attach the trap fitting to the sink waste in the same way as for a conventional trap. The stopped horizontal spigot on the washing machine trap is graded for different sizes of outlet hose; at the mark on the spigot corresponding to the diameter of the outlet hose supplied, cut off the end of the spigot with a trimming knife. Connect the end of the outlet hose to the open spigot with a jubilee clip.

In the installation shown, the supply pipes for the washing machine are teed off from the existing sink supply pipes and connected to the inlet hoses with compression fittings that incorporate shut-off valves.

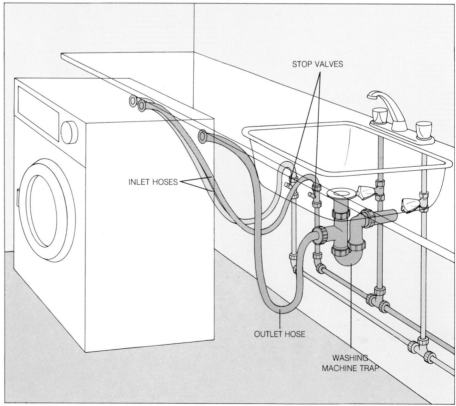

STOP VALVES

INLET HOSES

OUTLET HOSE

WASHING MACHINE TRAP

Picture Credits

The sources for the illustrations in this book are shown below. Credits for the pictures from left to right are separated by semi-colons, from top to bottom by dashes.

Cover, 6: Martin Brigdale. 8, 9: Drawings by Oxford Illustrators Ltd. 10: Drawings by Peter McGinn(2)—drawing by Oxford Illustrators Ltd. 11: Drawing by Oxford Illustrators Ltd.—drawing by Frederic F. Bigio from B-C Graphics—drawing by Peter McGinn. 12–17: Drawings by Oxford Illustrators Ltd. 18: Drawings by Oxford Illustrators Ltd.(3)—drawing by Gerry Gallagher. 19: Drawings by Gerry Gallagher. 20, 21: Drawings by Laszlo L. Bodrogi from Artograph Associates. 23: Drawings by Peter McGinn(3)—drawing by Oxford Illustrators Ltd. 24, 25: Drawings by Oxford Illustrators Ltd. 26: Drawings by Oxford Illustrators Ltd.(2)—drawing by Peter McGinn. 27: Drawing by Peter McGinn—drawing by Oxford Illustrators Ltd. 28: Drawings by Oxford Illustrators Ltd.(2)—drawing by Oxford Illustrators Ltd.; drawing by Peter McGinn. 29: Drawings by Dick Gage. 30: Drawing by Frederic F. Bigio from B-C Graphics. 31: Drawing by Frederic F. Bigio from B-C Graphics—drawing by Oxford Illustrators Ltd.—drawings by Frederic F. Bigio from B-C Graphics. 32: Drawing by Frederic F. Bigio from B-C Graphics—drawings by Oxford Illustrators Ltd. 33: Drawings by Oxford Illustrators Ltd. 34: Drawing by Oxford Illustrators Ltd.(top)—drawings by Frederic F. Bigio from B-C Graphics. 35: Drawing by Oxford Illustrators Ltd.—drawings by Frederic F. Bigio from B-C Graphics(3). 36: Fred Maroon. 38: Drawing by Oxford Illustrators Ltd. 39: Drawing by Adolph E. Brotman—drawings by Oxford Illustrators Ltd. 40–42: Drawings by Adolph E. Brotman. 43: Drawings by Oxford Illustrators Ltd. 44–47: Drawings by Ray Skibinski. 48–50: Drawings by Frederic F. Bigio from B-C Graphics. 51–56: Drawings by Oxford Illustrators Ltd. 57: Drawings by Vicki Vebell. 58–61: Drawings by Oxford Illustrators Ltd. 62–65: Drawings by Gerry Gallagher. 66: Drawings by Gerry Gallagher—drawing by Oxford Illustrators Ltd. 67: Drawings by Peter McGinn. 68: Drawings by Peter McGinn(2)—drawing by Oxford Illustrators Ltd. 69: Drawings by Oxford Illustrators Ltd. 70: Drawings by Vicki Vebell. 71: Drawings by Oxford Illustrators Ltd. 72: Martin Brigdale. 77: Drawing by Oxford Illustrators Ltd. 79–81: Drawings by Whitman Studios Inc. 82: Drawings by Vantage Art Inc. 83: Drawing by Vantage Art Inc.—drawing by Oxford Illustrators Ltd. 84, 85: Drawings by Oxford Illustrators Ltd. 86: Fil Hunter. 88: Drawing by Adolph E. Brotman. 89: Drawing by Adolph E. Brotman—drawing by Oxford Illustrators Ltd; drawing by Adolph E. Brotman. 90: Drawing by Adolph E. Brotman; drawing by Oxford Illustrators Ltd.—drawing by Oxford Illustrators Ltd. 91: Drawing by Adolph E. Brotman—drawing by Oxford Illustrators Ltd.—drawings by Adolph E. Brotman, except far right by Oxford Illustrators Ltd. 92: Drawings by Nicholas Fasciano. 93: Drawing by Nicholas Fasciano—drawings by Oxford Illustrators Ltd. 94: Drawing by Nicholas Fasciano. 95: Drawings by Oxford Illustrators Ltd. 96: Drawings by Nicholas Fasciano—drawing by Oxford Illustrators Ltd. 97: Drawings by Nicholas Fasciano. 98: Drawing by Nicholas Fasciano—drawing by Nicholas Fasciano; drawing by Great, Inc. 99: Drawings by Oxford Illustrators Ltd. 100: Drawing by Great, Inc.—drawing by Oxford Illustrators Ltd. 101–104: Drawings by Oxford Illustrators Ltd. 105: Drawing by Oxford Illustrators Ltd.—drawings by Peter McGinn. 106–113: Drawings by Oxford Illustrators Ltd. 114: Drawing by John Massey—drawing by John Massey; drawing by Oxford Illustrators Ltd. 115–118: Drawings by Oxford Illustrators Ltd. 119: Drawings by Oxford Illustrators Ltd.—drawings by Vicki Vebell. 120–123: Drawings by Oxford Illustrators Ltd.

Acknowledgements

The editors would like to extend special thanks to Susie Bicknell and Timothy Fraser, London. They also wish to thank the following: Alexandra Carlier, London; Warren Gadd, G & H Building Services, Otford, Kent; GEC-Xpelair Ltd., Birmingham; Mr. T.W. Hill, District Surveyor, Fulham and Hammersmith Borough Council, London; Hunter Building Products Ltd., London; Ideal Standard Ltd., Kingston upon Hull; Kentron Plastics Ltd., Gloucester; Marley Floors Ltd., Maidstone, Kent; Reject Tile Shop, London; Scandinavian Saunas, Wigan, Lancashire; Trent Valley Plastics Ltd., Burton-on-Trent, Staffs.

Index/Glossary

Included in this index are definitions of many of the technical terms used in this book. Page references in italics indicate an illustration of the subject mentioned.

Adhesives: for ceramic tiles, 22; for plaster laminate panelling, 33, *34*; for plastic laminate sheet, 30, *31*; for vinyl cove moulding, 20, *20*; for vinyl flooring, *19*

Airlocks (in pipework), curing, 113

Anti-siphon valve, 106; fitting to waste pipe, *106*

Axial fan, 52; installing, *53*

Ball-pein hammer: *hammer with one striking face shaped in the form of a hemisphere*; 116

Basin: mounting on partition wall, 100, *100*; fitting pedestal to, *100*; installing pop-up plug, 116, *118*; positioning in bathroom, 82, *83–84*; removing old, 88, *88–89*; installing supply pipes, *83, 85,* 108; support for, 100, *100*; attaching taps to, 116, *116*; tiling round pedestal, *26*; and vanity unit, 82, *85,* 100; laying vinyl flooring round pedestal, 14, *14–16*; installing waste fittings, 116, *117*; installing waste pipe, *83–85,* 102, *103–105,* 106, *107*

Baskets, sliding: installing in kitchen cabinets, 48, *51*

Bath: acrylic, 100; adjusting height of, *101*; boxing in, 67, *67–68*; breaking up cast-iron, *91*; cabinet extension to, *68–69*; fitting laminate panelling round, *35*; plastic, 100; installing pop-up plug, 116, *118*; positioning in bathroom, 82, *83–84*; removing old, 88, *90–91*; sizes, 73; soundproofing, 116; installing supply pipes, *83,* 108; supporting cradle for, 100, *101*; fixing taps to, 116, *116*; installing waste fittings, 116, *117*; installing waste pipe, *83–85,* 102, *103–105,* 106, *107*

Bathroom: installing accessories, 29, *29*; boxing in bath, 67, *67–68*; cabinet extension to bath, 67, *68–69*; carpeting for, 7; checking for damp in, 8; installing fan, 52, *53*; hanging mirrors, *70–71*; panelling walls with plastic laminate, *33–35*; partitioning, 73, 82, *85*; pipework, 82, *83–85,* *102–108*; planning new layout, 73, 82; planning plumbing, 73, *74–75,* 76, *77, 82–84*; positioning fixtures, 82, *83–85*; preparing walls and floor, 8, *9–11*; removing old basin, 88, *88–89*; removing old bath, 88, *90–91*; removing old W.C., 88, *90*; removing

walls, *92–93*; replacing subfloor, *12–13*; minimum size of, 73, 82; creating storage and counter space, 82, *84*; supports for fixtures, *100–101*; tiling floor, *24–26*; tiling walls, *27–28*; laying vinyl flooring, *14–21*; wet walls for, 82, 83, *84, 94–97*; wiring, 76

Battens: *strips of wood*; to increase thickness of worktop core, 40; making framework of, 33, *33*; for wet walls, 94, *94*

Bench: building for sauna, 65

Bending spring: *tool for bending pipes*; using, *110*

Bidet: installing pop-up plug, 116, *118*; fixing taps to, 116, *116*; installing waste fittings, 116, *117*; installing waste pipe, *83–85,* 102, *103–105,* 106, *107*

Block plane, using *7, 31*

Bolster: *cold chisel with broad blade*; using, *58, 59, 93, 95*

Boss connection: *PVC pipe connector used to join a waste pipe directly to a soil pipe*; *84,* 102; fitting into stack, *103*

Brackets, for pipework, 100, *100*; spacing between, *100*

Bricks, trimming, *59*

Building control officer, 75

Building regulations, 75

Butt joint: *formed by two pieces that come together but do not overlap*; 38, *43*

Cabinet extension to bath, 67, *68–69*

Cabinets, kitchen: installing fixed and sliding baskets, 48, *51*; building drawers, *49*; fastening together, *46*; fillet strips for, 44, *46*; installing glides, 48, *49*; hanging, 44, *44–45*; installing on floor, *46*; fitting retractable refuse bin, 48, *50*; removing old, 44; removing old shelves, 48, *48*; fitting pull-out saucepan rack, 48, *49*; reorganizing, 48; shimming for plumb, *37, 45*; installing swivelling tray, 48, *51*; adding vertical dividers, 48, *50*

Cap: *used to seal pipes temporarily*; capillary, *91*; compression, *91*; threaded, *91*

Capillary joint, 108; making, *110*

Carousel tray: installing in kitchen cabinet, 48, *51*

Carpeting, 7; edging for doorways, 21, *21*

Ceramic tiles: applying adhesive, 22, *24, 25, 28*; covering with plastic laminate, 30; cutting, 22, *23*; cutting border tiles, *26*; cutting corner tiles, *26*; drilling, *29*; for floors, 22; grouting, 22, *25, 26*; laying on floors, *24–26*; preparing surfaces for, 22; removing, *8*; repairing grout lines, *28*; replacing broken, *28*; setting in wall,

27–28; sizes, 22; spacer lugs, 22; for walls, 22

Chase, cutting a, *95*

Chipboard subfloor, 8; laying, 12, *13*; patching, *11*

Chipboard underlayment, 8; installing, *11*

Cistern, cold water, 76, 77

Cistern, W.C., installing, *120–121*

Cloakrooms, 73

Compression cap: *to seal pipes temporarily*; *91*

Compression fittings, 108; using, *109*

Condensation: reducing in kitchens and bathrooms, 52

Contact adhesives, 30; using, *31*

Cooker, *see* Hob; Oven

Cooker hood, 52; cleaning grease filter, 52; installing, *54–55*; replacing carbon filter, 52

Cornell University studies, 74

cPVC pipes: *pipes made with chlorinated polyvinyl chloride, which can withstand high temperatures*; 87, 91, 95, 108, 112, 114. *See also* Pipework

Cripple studs, 99

Cylinder, hot water, 76, 77

Damp, signs of, 8

Dishwasher: disconnecting drain hose, 89; positioning, 78; fitting trap to sink waste for, 122, *123*; installing waste pipe, 102, 106, *107*

Doors: mounting laminate panelling round, 35; installing thresholds, 21, *21*

Door sets: *prefabricated assembly of door and door jamb*; 99; installing, *99*

Double-pole fused isolating switch, 52

Drainage system: single-stack, 76, 77, 102; two-stack, 76, 102. *See also* Stacks; Waste pipes

Drain valves, 108; installing, *112*

Dry rot, 8

Ducts, extraction, 52; installing, *54, 55*; rerouting, 76

Elbow fittings, 108, 113; capping, *91*

Electricity: safety precautions in kitchens and bathrooms, 52, 81

Fan, extraction, 52; installing in exterior wall, *53*

Floor: choice of covering, 7; preparing subfloor for new covering, 8, *10. See also* Floorboards; Subfloor; Underlayment

Floorboards, tongue and groove, 8; laying, 12, *12–13*; patching, *11*; sanding, 8

Furring of pipes, 113

Metric Conversion Chart

Approximate equivalents—length

Millimetres to inches		Inches to millimetres	
1	$\frac{1}{32}$	$\frac{1}{32}$	1
2	$\frac{1}{16}$	$\frac{1}{16}$	2
3	$\frac{1}{8}$	$\frac{1}{8}$	3
4	$\frac{5}{32}$	$\frac{3}{16}$	5
5	$\frac{3}{16}$	$\frac{1}{4}$	6
6	$\frac{1}{4}$	$\frac{5}{16}$	8
7	$\frac{9}{32}$	$\frac{3}{8}$	10
8	$\frac{5}{16}$	$\frac{7}{16}$	11
9	$\frac{11}{32}$	$\frac{1}{2}$	13
10 (1cm)	$\frac{3}{8}$	$\frac{9}{16}$	14
11	$\frac{7}{16}$	$\frac{5}{8}$	16
12	$\frac{15}{32}$	$\frac{11}{16}$	17
13	$\frac{1}{2}$	$\frac{3}{4}$	19
14	$\frac{9}{16}$	$\frac{13}{16}$	21
15	$\frac{19}{32}$	$\frac{7}{8}$	22
16	$\frac{5}{8}$	$\frac{15}{16}$	24
17	$\frac{11}{16}$	1	25
18	$\frac{23}{32}$	2	51
19	$\frac{3}{4}$	3	76
20	$\frac{25}{32}$	4	102
25	1	5	127
30	$1\frac{3}{16}$	6	152
40	$1\frac{9}{16}$	7	178
50	$1\frac{15}{16}$	8	203
60	$2\frac{3}{8}$	9	229
70	$2\frac{3}{4}$	10	254
80	$3\frac{1}{8}$	11	279
90	$3\frac{9}{16}$	12 (1ft)	305
100	$3\frac{15}{16}$	13	330
200	$7\frac{7}{8}$	14	356
300	$11\frac{13}{16}$	15	381
400	$15\frac{3}{4}$	16	406
500	$19\frac{11}{16}$	17	432
600	$23\frac{5}{8}$	18	457
700	$27\frac{9}{16}$	19	483
800	$31\frac{1}{2}$	20	508
900	$35\frac{7}{16}$	24 (2ft)	610
1000 (1m)	$39\frac{3}{8}$	Yards to metres	

Metres to feet/inches		Yards to metres	
		1	0.914
2	6′ 7″	2	1.83
3	9′ 10″	3	2.74
4	13′ 1″	4	3.65
5	16′ 5″	5	4.57
6	19′ 8″	6	5.49
7	23′ 0″	7	6.40
8	26′ 3″	8	7.32
9	29′ 6″	9	8.23
10	32′ 10″	10	9.14
20	65′ 7″	20	18.29
50	164′ 0″	50	45.72
100	328′ 7″	100	91.44

Conversion factors

Length

1 millimetre (mm)	= 0.0394 in
1 centimetre (cm)/10 mm	= 0.3937 in
1 metre/100 cm	= 39.37 in/3.281 ft/1.094 yd
1 kilometre (km)/1000 metres	= 1093.6 yd/0.6214 mile
1 inch (in)	= 25.4 mm/2.54 cm
1 foot (ft)/12 in	= 304.8 mm/30.48 cm/0.3048 metre
1 yard (yd)/3 ft	= 914.4 mm/91.44 cm/0.9144 metre
1 mile/1760 yd	= 1609.344 metres/1.609 km

Area

1 square centimetre (sq cm)/ 100 square millimetres (sq mm)	= 0.155 sq in
1 square metre (sq metre)/10,000 sq cm	= 10.764 sq ft/1.196 sq yd
1 are/100 sq metres	= 119.60 sq yd/0.0247 acre
1 hectare (ha)/100 ares	= 2.471 acres/0.00386 sq mile
1 square inch (sq in)	= 645.16 sq mm/6.4516 sq cm
1 square foot (sq ft)/144 sq in	= 929.03 sq cm
1 square yard (sq yd)/9 sq ft	= 8361.3 sq cm/0.8361 sq metre
1 acre/4840 sq yd	= 4046.9 sq metres/0.4047 ha
1 square mile/640 acres	= 259 ha/2.59 sq km

Volume

1 cubic centimetre (cu cm)/ 1000 cubic millimetres (cu mm)	= 0.0610 cu in
1 cubic decimetre (cu dm)/1000 cu cm	= 61.024 cu in/0.0353 cu ft
1 cubic metre/1000 cu dm	= 35.3146 cu ft/1.308 cu yd
1 cu cm	= 1 millilitre (ml)
1 cu dm	= 1 litre see **Capacity**
1 cubic inch (cu in)	= 16.3871 cu cm
1 cubic foot (cu ft)/1728 cu in	= 28.3168 cu cm/0·0283 cu metre
1 cubic yard (cu yd)/27 cu ft	= 0.7646 cu metre

Capacity

1 litre	= 1.7598 pt/0.8799 qt/0.22 gal
1 pint (pt)	= 0.568 litre
1 quart (qt)	= 1.137 litres
1 gallon (gal)	= 4.546 litres

Weight

1 gram (g)	= 0.035 oz
1 kilogram (kg)/1000 g	= 2.20 lb/35.2 oz
1 tonne/1000 kg	= 2204.6 lb/0.9842 ton
1 ounce (oz)	= 28.35 g
1 pound (lb)	= 0.4536 kg
1 ton	= 1016 kg

Pressure

1 gram per square metre (g/metre^2)	= 0.0292 oz/sq yd
1 gram per square centimetre (g/cm^2)	= 0.226 oz/sq in
1 kilogram per square centimetre (kg/cm^2)	= 14.226 lb/sq in
1 kilogram per square metre (kg/metre^2)	= 0.205 lb/sq ft
1 pound per square foot (lb/ft^2)	= 4.882 kg/metre^2
1 pound per square inch (lb/in^2)	= 703.07 kg/metre^2
1 ounce per square yard (oz/yd^2)	= 33.91 g/metre^2
1 ounce per square foot (oz/ft^2)	= 305.15 g/metre^2

Temperature

To convert °F to °C, subtract 32, then divide by 9 and multiply by 5

To convert °C to °F, divide by 5 and multiply by 9, then add 32

Phototypeset by Tradespools Limited, Frome, Somerset
Printed in Spain by Artes Gráficas Toledo, S.A.
D. L. TO:395-1985